Cooking in Season

Cooking in Season
by Christine Brady

ALAN CRACKNELL

ELM TREE BOOKS · HAMISH HAMILTON · LONDON

First published in Great Britain 1977
by Elm Tree Books
90 Great Russell Street, London WC1B 3PT

Copyright © 1977 by Christine Brady

SBN 241 89451 4

Illustrations by Alan Cracknell

Filmset and printed in Great Britain by
BAS Printers Limited, Wallop, Hampshire

Contents

Introduction

This is a book for people who like cooking—for people who find it fun and relaxing yet don't have much time to spare.

It makes good sense to cook with foods in season. Not only are the fruits and vegetables at the peak of their condition but towards the end of their season they're at their cheapest too. Sometimes there are gluts, when the supply exceeds demand, and that is the time to leap in and buy large quantities to make chutneys and jams. If you have joined the growing army of home gardeners, it is even more essential to know what to do with every single pea or apple that comes your way after all the previous hard work.

All my shopping for the recipe-testing in this book was carried out in an ordinary London street market, and the recipes were devised using the foods in season at the time, when they were at their cheapest. All the recipes use fresh foods. The only exception to this is canned tomatoes, because their flavour is unique and you don't need to go to the trouble of skinning them first.

With meat, too, there are seasons when you can buy well. Basically it's the law of supply and demand again, so when everyone is after the same meat it is probably at its dearest. Look out for good-buy guides in the consumer shopping columns of your newspapers. As so many people don't know how to use the cheaper cuts of meat, the demand is less and so they usually represent very good value. This applies to offal such as hearts, to rabbit and to stewing lamb, as well as good old stewing steak. As for fish, I've never understood why sprats and mussels are so cheap as their value and taste are superb. Cod and haddock, unfortunately, have become a treat for most of us, but coley and whiting make good substitutes.

In the interests of economy I have limited each recipe that called for cream to 125 ml ($\frac{1}{4}$ pint). It seems to me that any more is bordering on the extravagant, and one can get much the same results as 250 ml ($\frac{1}{2}$ pint) cream by adding an egg white to a 125-ml ($\frac{1}{4}$-pint) carton before whisking. The whipping consistency is very much the same, although piping would be more difficult.

One of the easiest ways to enjoy cooking is to be relaxed about it. Even if you make a mistake it can usually be remedied. This I learned during a very pleasurable three-month course at the Cordon Bleu in London, many years ago. If our cakes tumbled into pieces out of the tin, we were shown how deftly to sandwich them together with butter icing or jam, and to use perhaps a fraction more decoration on top so that no one would ever know of our mishap.

If anything sticks to the bottom of the pan and is in danger of burning just tip the remainder into another pan and forget scraping the bottom but leave the old pan to soak and no harm should come to your meal.

Recipe measures used here are in metric; the imperial measurements are in brackets. It is important to follow one set of measurements or the other and not float between the two. This is because the metric is not an exact equivalent and the results will be slightly less in volume. Where equivalents shown appear to be inconsistent this has been done deliberately to maintain correct proportions, for example in making pastry. Unless otherwise stated, each recipe will make enough for 4 people.

All of the recipes in this book are easy—some are rather glamorous and will impress your guests, others have a more homely style that will give a much-needed lift to a mid-week meal or supper round the fire. They have all been devised with a minimum of ingredients as there is nothing in the world as annoying as deciding to make something only to discover that half the ingredients have to be bought specially. As far as possible I have tried to remember that it will most likely be poor old you who washes up afterwards, and I have kept utensils to a minimum.

Some of my own favourite pots and pans at home have made me feel almost a cheat in this context. I could never be without my black cast-iron pan, which nearly broke my back as I carried it from the north of Finland after a holiday. It's heavy to lift, but marvellous to be able to use it on top of the stove and then to put it into the oven. Those of you with a similar top-of-stove-and-into-the-oven pan will be able to ignore the instructions to transfer ingredients from a frying pan to an ovenproof casserole.

For speed there's just nothing like an electric blender which can also help you to use every ingredient down to the last crumb or drop. Another gadget I wouldn't be without is a Mouli. Mine came from a hardware store in mid-France at least fifteen years ago, although of course one can buy them quite easily over here now. This particular version has three plates with varying-sized holes so that the thickness of the purée can vary. The joy of using it is that you can cook fruit such as apples with peel and core and get far more of the most lovely tasting purée as a result.

If you are using an ordinary sieve you will do very well, but the food may have to be cooked a little more than if you are using a blender. Use a nylon sieve if the food is likely to discolour from being pushed through a metal one. Other than that the recipes here call for nothing more than a whisk (electric or a balloon type is best), a wooden spoon, a spatula for scooping up the very last drop of any mixture and a variety of sharp knives.

Always take a little extra time to present your meal with care. The sprig of mint or chopped parsley or grated cheese browned under the grill can give a meal eye appeal which lifts it right out of the 'ordinary' class and gets the digestive juices working at once. Similarly, choose the accompanying vegetables with colour in mind and make the most of the bright orange of carrots, the brilliant red of tomatoes and the lovely deep green of spinach to add colour to the dish.

Above all, leave yourself enough energy and time to serve the meal well, and finally sit down and enjoy your own good cooking. After all, there's nothing like it!

As the evenings slowly lengthen and the first watery sun shines through the cloud, our tastes in food slowly and imperceptibly change. Almost without realising it, we leave behind the deep dark browns of warming winter casseroles and begin to prepare dishes that are lighter in colour and texture. As spring gets its grip on us we take stock of ourselves and sorrowfully acknowledge that we've added a pound or two to our hips and we'll 'have to do something about it' very soon.

Slowly as the weather changes it's possible to ignore some of the more fattening parts of our diet, to leave out just one potato, or serve meals on smaller plates—which has a wonderful psychological effect if we're trying to slim the family without them knowing. Spring is a time when we want to feel as well as look better. Many of the herbal country soups are claimed to 'do us good'; for starters try Nettle Soup or Chervil Soup, beloved by French housewives.

It's still possible to cook using cheaper cuts of meat, although you can't disguise them as well as you can in a winter casserole. Liver is always a good buy and don't neglect fish such as whiting or the perennial bargain, chicken. Turkeys are often available around Easter time, and turkey meat can be used instead of chicken in any of the recipes which follow.

The first salad vegetables come into the shops now and although many families claim not to like salads greatly, it's surprising how well they go with meat dishes, served on a side plate, instead of a hot vegetable.

Fruit is rather sparse at this time of the year except for rhubarb, which is why I have included several recipes using this lovely inexpensive food. Try not to use too much sugar with it, especially if you are trying to slim—use honey to sweeten instead.

Eggs are probably at their cheapest in late spring, so make the most of the bargain and serve omelettes, baked eggs and egg custards.

Starters

Chervil Soup

This soup is popular in France but not as well known here. It's claimed by herbalists to be a blood purifier and spring tonic, and its delicate flavour makes a change from more traditional soups.

25 g (1 oz) butter
3 tablespoons fresh chopped chervil or green-dried
1 medium-sized potato
black pepper and salt
750 ml (1½ pints) chicken or vegetable stock
1 tablespoon cream (or top of the milk)

Melt the butter in a pan, add the chopped chervil and grated potato. Sauté for a few minutes, then season well. Add stock, bring to a boil and simmer gently for 20 minutes. Add cream or top of the milk just before serving.

Celery Soup

1 head celery
1 medium-sized onion
sprig parsley
25 g (1 oz) butter
blade mace
bay leaf
1.2 litres (2 pints) stock or water
12.5 g (½ oz) cornflour
125 ml (¼ pint) milk

Wash the celery well and chop it into small pieces using as much of the stalk as you can. Chop the onion and the parsley finely.

Melt the butter in a saucepan and gently fry the onion. Add the celery, mace, bay leaf, stock and parsley. Bring to the boil, then simmer for 15–20 minutes. Liquidise in a blender or rub through a sieve.

Blend the cornflour with a little of the milk to make a smooth paste. Add the rest of the milk and pour the mixture into the soup. Reheat to boiling point to thicken, stirring all the time. Adjust seasoning and serve.
Serves 6

Onion Soup

450 g (1 lb) small onions
25 g (1 oz) butter
1 tablespoon sugar
750 ml (1½ pints) brown stock
seasoning

For the garnish:
2 slices bread
2 slices cheese to cover

Peel the onions and cut them into slices. Melt the butter in a saucepan and fry the onions gently. Sprinkle sugar over and allow to cook very gently until onions are brown. Add stock and seasoning. Bring to a boil and simmer for about 30 minutes. Pour into heat-proof soup dishes. Cut each slice of bread in four and cover with cheese. Float two pieces on each soup dish and brown under grill until cheese is bubbling. Serve at once.

Nettle Soup

Nettle soup is claimed by country folk to be an excellent tonic, and it's certainly inexpensive to make. Only make the soup from young nettles in the spring.

150 g (6 oz) nettles
1 medium-sized onion
1 medium-sized potato
25 g (1 oz) butter
salt
pepper
750 ml (1½ pints) chicken stock

Use rubber gloves when you pick the nettles, which should be young and free from sprays or insecticide. Strip leaves from stalks and wash well.

Put them into a saucepan with a close-fitting lid and cook without water over a low heat for about ten minutes. Shake the pan from time to time to prevent leaves sticking. Chop leaves finely—the sting has gone once they have been cooked.

Chop the onion finely. Peel the potato and chop it into small pieces. Melt the butter in a pan and fry onion and potato. Season and add stock. Bring to the boil, add chopped nettles and simmer for 15 minutes.

Press through a fine sieve or use a blender if you have one. Serve at once.

Root Vegetable Soup

Vary the vegetables to ring the changes.

450 g (1 lb) root vegetables such as 2 carrots, 2 parsnips, 1 potato
1 medium-sized onion
25 g (1 oz) butter
500 ml (1 pint) water
salt
pepper
1 bay leaf
250 ml (½ pint) milk
grated nutmeg

Clean, scrape and finely chop the root vegetables. Chop the onion and fry it in the melted butter until soft. Add chopped vegetables and fry gently for a few more minutes. Add the water, salt, pepper and bay leaf. Bring to a boil and simmer for about 25 minutes, then press through a sieve or put in a blender if you have one. Pour in the milk, reheat, and adjust seasoning. Sprinkle with grated nutmeg just before serving.

Kidney Soup

This is a well flavoured meat soup that's not expensive to make.

225 g (8 oz) ox kidney
little flour
salt and pepper
2 medium-sized onions
25 g (1 oz) butter
500 ml (1 pint) water
125 ml (¼ pint) milk

Cut up the ox kidney into small pieces and roll in seasoned flour. Chop onions finely. Melt the butter in a pan and fry chopped onions until soft but not brown. Add the kidney pieces and continue to fry for five minutes. Pour over the water. Season, bring to the boil, then simmer for 15 minutes. Blend in a liquidiser, or put through a sieve. Add milk, reheat, adjust seasoning and serve.

Savoury Eggs

This is one of my favourite starters, but you can easily serve double quantities for a supper dish.

4 eggs
50 g (2 oz) butter
2 tablespoons chopped parsley and thyme mixed
seasoning
225 g (½ lb) tomatoes

For the sauce:
25 g (1 oz) butter
25 g (1 oz) flour
250 ml (½ pint) milk
50 g (2 oz) grated Cheddar cheese

Hard boil the eggs. Shell them, cut in half lengthwise and remove the yolks. Mix the yolks with the butter, the finely chopped herbs and seasoning until well blended. Pile back into the egg whites. Cut the tomatoes into thin slices and use them to line the bottom of a greased shallow ovenproof dish. Place the eggs on top.

Make a sauce by melting the butter and removing the pan from the heat. Stir in the flour, then add the milk, stirring well to avoid lumps. Return the pan to the heat and bring to a boil, stirring continuously, until the sauce thickens. Season well and spoon over the eggs. Cover the pan with buttered greaseproof paper and reheat in a warm oven, 160°C (325°F)/Gas 3, for 15 minutes. Remove the greaseproof paper, sprinkle grated cheese over the savoury eggs and brown under the grill before serving.

Eggs Baked with Tarragon Cream

A delicate and delicious starter for a spring dinner party.

4 tablespoons double cream
2 tablespoons chopped tarragon
4 eggs
salt
pepper

Preheat oven to 160°C (325°F)/Gas 3. Butter four ramekin dishes. Into each one, put a tablespoon of cream and a generous sprinkling of tarragon. Save some to sprinkle on top when serving. Break an egg into each dish, season with salt and pepper.

Place ramekin dishes in a baking tin and half fill the tin with hot water. Bake in the centre of the oven for about 10 minutes. The whites should be just set. They must be eaten while the yolk is still soft to make the most of the delicate flavour. Sprinkle the top with remaining tarragon just before serving.

Puff Pastry Squares

This number of squares will serve 4 people as a substantial starter or as a light main meal when served with salad.

For the pastry:
225 g (8 oz) plain flour
¼ teaspoon salt
225 g (8 oz) butter
¼ teaspoon lemon juice
cold water to mix
1 egg beaten with ½ teaspoon salt

For the filling:
50 g (2 oz) cooked diced chicken
50 g (2 oz) diced ham
2 tablespoons chopped parsley
50 g (2 oz) butter
50 g (2 oz) flour
250 ml (½ pint) milk
salt and pepper

Sift the flour and salt into a bowl. Take one quarter of the butter and cut it into small pieces. Rub the butter into the flour with your fingertips until the mixture resembles fine breadcrumbs. Add the lemon juice and enough cold water to make a fine dough. Cover with waxed or greaseproof paper and refrigerate for 15 minutes.

Put the remaining butter between greaseproof paper and press with a rolling pin into an oblong about 2 cm (¾ in) thick. Roll out the dough to 1.5 cm (½ in) thick and place the unwrapped butter in the middle. Fold over the pastry and seal all the edges to make a parcel. Refrigerate again for 15 minutes.

Place the dough, folds to the underside, on a floured board and roll gently to make a rectangle. Fold into three, like an envelope, then turn at right angles. Roll out again, fold in three, turn at right angles and roll out again. Refrigerate. Repeat whole process twice more so that the pastry is rolled out six times in all. Great care must be taken in rolling to keep the edges square or the pastry will rise unevenly. Roll out pastry to 1 cm (⅓ in) thick. Cut into eight 7.5-cm (3-in) squares. With the point of a knife score a square about 1.5 cm (½ in) inside the edge. Wet a baking sheet by pouring water over it, then turning it over to pour away excess. Stand the pastry squares on the sheet and refrigerate again for about 10 minutes. Preheat oven to 220°C (425°F)/Gas 7. Brush pastry squares with beaten egg to which ½ teaspoon of salt has been added. Bake for 20–25 minutes until golden brown. Remove from baking sheet and allow the pastry to cool. With a spoon hollow out the centre of each pastry square. Be careful to keep each centre whole, as you will replace them later.

To make the filling, mix chicken, ham and chopped parsley together. Melt the butter in a pan, draw off the heat and stir in the flour. Gradually add milk, stirring continually. Return to heat and beat vigorously until the mixture just bubbles. Add chopped chicken, ham, season well. Fill the pastry shells with the mixture, top with the pastry squares and reheat in a gentle oven, 160°C (325°F)/Gas 3.

By using the same basic binding sauce, a variety of fillings can be used—any flavoured cooked meat, or fish. If you use scrambled egg with prawns, the pastry cases should be reheated unfilled and the egg added just before serving.

Makes 8 squares

Ham and Mushroom Bake

Buy the sort of ham that doesn't fall apart when you're rolling it up.

225 g (8 oz) mushrooms
50 g (2 oz) butter
4 cloves garlic
3 tablespoons tomato purée
seasoning
8 slices thinly cut ham

Chop the mushrooms into thick slices. Melt the butter in a pan, add the chopped garlic and mushrooms. Fry gently. Remove the pan from the heat, stir in tomato purée and season. Put a dessertspoon of the mixture into each ham slice and roll up. Arrange in a shallow ovenproof dish and pour any remaining mixture on top. Cover with greaseproof paper and heat in the oven, 160°C (325°F)/Gas 3, for 15–20 minutes. Serve with toast.

Herrings with Mushroom Stuffing

This could easily become a main meal according to the size of the fish.

4 small herrings
100 g (4 oz) mushrooms
50 g (2 oz) butter
50 g (2 oz) fresh breadcrumbs
2 teaspoons chopped chives
salt
pepper

Clean and gut the herrings. Chop the mushrooms. Melt the butter in a pan, stir in the breadcrumbs and fry gently. Add mushrooms and continue to fry for a few minutes. Add chopped chives, and season well. Fill the cavity of each herring with the stuffing. Place in an ovenproof dish, cover with foil or buttered paper and cook for 30 minutes at 180°C (350°F)/Gas 4.

Serve with thinly cut brown bread and butter.

Mixed Spring Salad

Salads make excellent first courses, and this crunchy combination is particularly delicious. Serve double quantities as a main course for lunch.

100 g (4 oz) raisins
100 g (4 oz) dried apricots
3 tablespoons oil
2 tablespoons herb or cider vinegar
pinch mustard
salt and pepper
2 red-skinned apples
1 banana
juice of 1 lemon
1 medium-sized onion
3 sticks celery
50 g (2 oz) walnuts (shelled)
1 green pepper
5–6 lettuce leaves

Combine the raisins and the dried apricots in a bowl. Make a French dressing by thoroughly mixing the oil, vinegar, mustard, salt and pepper. Pour the dressing over the raisins and apricots, cover, and leave overnight.

The next day, prepare the rest of the ingredients just before you wish to serve the salad. Cut and core the apples, but leave them in their skins. Slice the banana and sprinkle lemon juice over the apples and banana to prevent discolouring. Grate the onion, chop the celery and walnuts. De-seed the pepper and cut it into small strips. Combine all the ingredients and mix together well.

To serve, arrange the washed lettuce leaves in a bowl and pile the salad in the middle.

Main Courses

Breast of Lamb with Apricot and Rice Stuffing

50 g (2 oz) dried apricots
2 medium-sized onions
2 tablespoons cooking oil
50 g (2 oz) long grain rice
½ teaspoon turmeric
½ teaspoon cumin seeds
salt and pepper
250 ml (½ pint) water
25 g (1 oz) sultanas
2 tablespoons chopped parsley
2 breasts of lamb

Soak the apricots in water overnight. Next day, chop onion finely and fry gently in oil until soft but not brown. Add the rice and fry for 2–3 minutes, then add the turmeric, cumin seeds and seasoning. Chop the apricots and add to the rice with water. Cook gently until the liquid has been absorbed. Add sultanas and chopped parsley. Stir in well and leave to cool.

Chine the breasts of lamb so that they can be easily carved into pieces when cooked. Lay one breast of lamb in the bottom of a baking tin and cover with the stuffing. Place the other breast of lamb on top. Brush with oil and cover with buttered greaseproof paper. Cook at 190°C (375°F)/Gas 5 for 1½ hours.

Nutty Lamb Chops

Vegetables can be cooked in the oven at the same time as this lamb dish, so that oven heat isn't wasted. Cook carrots, swedes or potatoes in a covered casserole by pouring over boiling water before putting them in the oven. Cut into fairly small pieces, they will be ready at the same time as the lamb.

4 lamb chump chops
peanut butter
1 orange

Preheat oven to 180°C (350°F)/Gas 4. Spread each chop very thickly with peanut butter, place them on a baking tray and cook for 25–30 minutes.

Peel the orange and cut it into segments. Just before serving the chops arrange orange segments over the top.

Lamb Arabesque

100 g (4 oz) dried apricots
shoulder of lamb about 1.5 kg (3½ lb)
1 tablespoon cooking oil
2 cloves garlic
1 teaspoon cinnamon
1 tablespoon flour
salt and pepper
375 ml (¾ pint) chicken stock
1 tablespoon brown sugar

Soak the apricots in water overnight or for at least 2–3 hours. Cut the meat cleanly from the bone and dice into cubes about 5 cm (2 in). Heat the oil in a pan and fry the meat with chopped garlic, cinnamon, flour and seasoning. Stir with a wooden spoon as the meat browns. Add stock, bring to a boil, cover with lid then simmer very gently for about an hour. Cut apricot halves in half again and, with the sugar, stir them into the meat mixture. Continue cooking for a further 15 minutes. Serve with plain boiled rice.

Use long grain rice, allowing 50 g (2 oz) per person. Half fill a saucepan with water, bring to boil, add 1 teaspoon salt and pour in the rice. Stir with a fork to prevent sticking. Allow to boil fairly fast with the lid off for 12 minutes. If the rice absorbs all the water, add more hot water from a kettle. Test to see if rice is cooked by removing two or three grains and biting them. It should be soft but still have a 'bite'.

Empty rice into a sieve and pour boiling water over it to remove the starch. Serve at once, or spread out on a baking tray and put in a low oven to keep hot.
Serves 6–8

Ragout of Lamb

½ leg lamb
2 tablespoons cooking oil
2 cloves garlic
25 g (1 oz) flour
salt
pepper
500 ml (1 pint) water
selection of onions, carrots, potato, swede, turnip
1 green pepper

Bone the lamb and cut the meat into cubes about 5 cm (2 in). Heat the oil and add the chopped garlic. Roll meat in seasoned flour and fry, browning all over to seal in the juices. Add water, cover the pan, bring to the boil, then simmer gently for one hour. Prepare the vegetables, cutting them into medium-sized pieces. De-seed pepper and chop into rings. Add all the vegetables and cook for a further 35 minutes.

Curried Lamb in Choux Pastry

Don't be put off at the thought of tackling choux pastry. It is really very easy and delicious when served with savoury fillings. This recipe is an excellent way to use left-over lamb.

For the choux pastry:
125 ml ($\frac{1}{4}$ pint) water
50 g (2 oz) butter
62.5 g (2$\frac{1}{2}$ oz) plain flour
2 standard eggs

For the curried lamb filling:
325 g (12 oz) cooked lamb
1 tablespoon curry powder
few drops Soy sauce
25 g (1 oz) sultanas
little stock if necessary
1 tablespoon chopped parsley

Preheat oven to 200°C (400°F)/Gas 6. Put the water and butter in a pan and heat to boiling. Remove from heat and pour in all the flour at once. Beat vigorously with a wooden spoon until the mixture is smooth and leaves the sides of the pan. Allow to cool a little. Beat the eggs together. When the mixture has cooled, add beaten egg, a little at a time, beating hard. The mixture should be glossy and stiff when the egg has been absorbed.

Cut the lamb into small pieces and mix with curry powder, Soy sauce and sultanas. Moisten with a little stock if the meat is dry.

Carefully butter a 17.5-cm (7-in) pie dish, then spread the choux pastry around the edge, using the back of a spoon. Pile the lamb in the centre. Cover the lamb with buttered paper, leaving the pastry uncovered, and cook for 30 minutes.

Just before serving sprinkle the centre with chopped parsley.

Lamb in Pastry

½ leg of lamb
2 large sprigs fresh rosemary (or 1 tablespoon dried)
25 g (1 oz) lard

For the pastry:
300 g (12 oz) plain flour
1 teaspoon salt
75 g (3 oz) lard
75 g (3 oz) butter
little milk

To remove the bone from the leg of lamb, use a sharp filleting knife and
ease it out gently. The butcher will do this for you if you give him
notice. Place the sprigs of rosemary inside the cavity and re-roll to shape.
Preheat the oven to 190°C (375°F)/Gas 5. Heat 25 g (1 oz) lard in a
baking tin. Stand the meat in the pan, baste it, then cook it in the oven
for 30 minutes. Remove and allow to cool.

Sieve the flour and salt into a bowl. Cut the fat into small pieces and
rub it into the flour until the mixture resembles fine breadcrumbs. Add
enough water to make a firm dough. Roll out until large enough to cover
the lamb. Put the lamb in the middle of the pastry, wrap the pastry
completely around it, and seal the edges by pinching them together with
a little cold water. Brush with milk.

Return the lamb to the oven and continue to cook at the same
temperature for 1 hour.

Beef and Bacon Casserole

2 medium-sized onions
2 tablespoons oil
225 g (8 oz) smoked bacon in one piece
450 g (1 lb) minced beef
seasoning
1 225-g (8-oz) can tomatoes
2 bay leaves
dash Worcestershire sauce
50 g (2 oz) fresh breadcrumbs
50 g (2 oz) grated cheese

Chop the onions and fry in the oil until soft but not brown. Cut the bacon
into 5-cm (2-in) pieces and fry with the onion, then add the minced beef
and brown gently. Season well, add the tomatoes and bay leaves. Sprinkle
in a little Worcestershire sauce. Transfer to a casserole, cover, and cook in

warm oven, 160°C (325°F)/Gas 3, for forty minutes. Uncover the pan and sprinkle breadcrumbs and grated cheese over the top. Turn the oven up to 180°C (350°F)/Gas 4 and cook for a further 30 minutes. Crisp the top under a hot grill before serving.

Calypso Beef Stew

2 medium-sized onions
1 green pepper
2 chillies or 1 teaspoon chilli powder
450 g (1 lb) stewing beef
2 tablespoons cooking oil
2 cloves garlic
1 teaspoon ginger
1 225-g (8-oz) can tomatoes
125 ml (¼ pint) beef stock
seasoning

Finely chop the onions. De-seed the pepper and chop into strips, and de-seed the chillies. Cut the beef into small pieces about 5 cm (2 in) square. Heat the oil in a pan and fry the onion until soft but not coloured. Remove the onion and use to cover the bottom of a greased ovenproof casserole. Fry the meat with the chopped garlic, sprinkling the ginger into the mixture as it cooks. Transfer the meat to the casserole with the pepper and chillies or chilli powder. Add the tomatoes and beef stock. Season well. Cook at 180°C (350°F)/Gas 4 for 2 hours.

Quick Mince Hash

2 medium-sized onions
25 g (1 oz) cooking fat
450 (1 lb) minced beef
2 dessertspoons Worcestershire sauce
2 dessertspoons tomato purée
125 ml (¼ pint) water
50 g (2 oz) sultanas
salt and pepper
225 g (8 oz) quick-cooking macaroni

Chop the onions finely. Heat the fat in a saucepan and fry the onions until soft but not brown. Add minced beef and fry until brown, stirring with a wooden spoon to prevent sticking. Add Worcestershire sauce, tomato purée and water, stirring well to blend. Add sultanas and season. Cover tightly and cook on a low heat for 15 minutes.

   In another pan, cook the macaroni according to the directions on the packet. Drain when cooked, stir into mince and serve at once.

Duck in Orange

1 teaspoon salt
¼ teaspoon pepper
½ teaspoon caraway seeds
1 tablespoon lemon juice
1 duck, about 2 kg (4½ lb) in weight
3 tablespoons vegetable oil
3 tablespoons orange marmalade

Blend the salt, pepper, caraway seeds and lemon juice together. Brush the liquid over duck and leave to stand for 2 hours.

Preheat oven to 190°C (375°F)/Gas 5. Heat the oil in roasting pan and put in the duck, breast side down. Place in the oven and after 15 minutes turn duck right side up and spoon over the marmalade.

Cook for a further hour.

Honeyed Chicken

50 g (2 oz) butter
2 tablespoons clear honey
2 teaspoons curry powder
salt
pepper
4 chicken joints

Preheat oven to 190°C (375°F)/Gas 5. Melt the butter in a saucepan, add honey and curry powder and seasoning. Stir until blended.

Put the chicken joints in a shallow ovenproof dish and pour the sauce over them so that each joint is well coated. Cook for about 30–35 minutes in the oven, basting frequently.

Serve with plain boiled rice and a spicy chutney.

Chicken with Peanut Butter

3 medium-sized onions
2 tablespoons vegetable oil
4 chicken joints
1 400-g (14-oz) can tomatoes
salt
pepper
1 tablespoon tomato ketchup
2 tablespoons peanut butter

Chop the onions finely and fry them in the oil until soft but not brown. Add the chicken and fry on all sides. Add the tomatoes and 125 ml (¼ pint) water. Season, add ketchup and simmer for 30 minutes. Take a little liquid from the pan, blend with the peanut butter and return, stirring, to the pan. Continue cooking for a further 15–20 minutes. Keep on a very low flame and only add more water to prevent sticking.

Oriental Chicken

2 tablespoons Soy sauce
juice of 1 lemon
½ teaspoon ground ginger
4 large chicken joints
3 medium-sized onions
2 tablespoons vegetable oil
25 g (1 oz) flour
salt and pepper

Mix the Soy sauce, lemon juice and ground ginger together. Put the chicken joints in an ovenproof dish, spoon the sauce over them and leave to marinate for 2 hours.

Preheat the oven to 190°C (375°F)/Gas 5. Slice the onions and fry them gently in the hot oil until soft. Drain the chicken joints, reserving the marinade, and coat them in seasoned flour. Remove onion slices from the frying pan and put them in the ovenproof dish. Fry the chicken joints until brown on both sides, then return them to the dish with the onions and spoon the marinade over them. Cover and cook in the oven for 35–40 minutes, depending on the size of the joints.

Serve with plain boiled rice.

Spring Fancy Chicken

An ideal way to use leftover chicken.

450 g (1 lb) cooked chicken
bunch spring onions
2 red apples
50 g (2 oz) butter
50 g (2 oz) flour
250 ml (½ pint) chicken stock
salt
pepper
1 tablespoon chopped parsley

Cut the cooked chicken into small bite-sized pieces. Trim spring onions and cut into 2.5-cm (1-in) lengths, using as much of the green as possible. Wipe the apples and cut into dice, but do not peel.

Melt the butter in a saucepan, remove from heat and stir in the flour. Gradually add the chicken stock. Return to heat and stir vigorously until sauce has thickened. Stir in chicken, onions, apples, and season well. Cover the pan and cook over a very low heat until mixture is hot through. Alternatively, transfer to an ovenproof dish and reheat in a low oven, 140°C (275°F)/Gas 1, for 15–20 minutes.

Pile the mixture on a plate and serve surrounded with boiled rice. Sprinkle with parsley just before serving.

Tarragon Veal

Tarragon and veal seem to be made for each other in this beautifully flavoured dish.

4 veal fillets each weighing about 150 g (6 oz)
2 cloves garlic
2 medium-sized onions
25 g (1 oz) butter
seasoning
100 g (4 oz) mushrooms
125 ml (¼ pint) stock
2 tablespoons cream
1 tablespoon chopped tarragon

Flatten the fillets with a rolling pin, and rub both sides of each fillet with garlic. Chop the onions finely and fry them in butter until soft but not brown. Add the veal and cook on both sides briefly until meat is sealed. Season well. Cut the mushrooms into slices and add to the pan together with the stock. Cover and cook for 15 minutes. Remove veal fillets and keep them hot. Add the cream to the sauce, blending it well, and heat but do not boil. Pour the sauce over the fillets and sprinkle with chopped tarragon just before serving.

Caraway Veal

450 g (1 lb) pie veal
50 g (2 oz) flour
salt and pepper
2 medium-sized onions
2 tablespoons oil
1 teaspoon caraway seeds
500 ml (1 pint) chicken stock
1 teaspoon paprika
1 tablespoon tomato purée
100 g (4 oz) mushrooms

Cut the pie veal into even cubes about 5 cm (2 in). Add salt and pepper to flour and roll the meat in it to coat each piece. Chop the onions finely and fry them in the oil until soft but not coloured. Add meat and continue to fry, stirring with a wooden spoon. When the veal is lightly browned, add the caraway seeds, stock, paprika and tomato purée and stir well. Bring to a boil, then turn down the heat and simmer gently for one hour. Slice the mushrooms and add them to the pan and continue to cook very gently for a further 25 minutes.

Mackerel and Spinach Flan

For the flan:
150 g (6 oz) wholemeal flour
½ teaspoon salt
75 g (3 oz) butter
25 g (1 oz) finely chopped walnuts
1 egg
water to mix

For the filling:
1 large mackerel (or a large can of mackerel)
450 g (1 lb) spinach
knob butter
little grated nutmeg
50 g (2 oz) grated cheese

Preheat oven to 190°C (375°F)/Gas 5. Sift the flour and salt into bowl. Rub in the butter with your fingertips until the mixture resembles fine breadcrumbs. Add the finely chopped walnuts. Beat the egg until yolk and white are thoroughly mixed, then add to dry ingredients with sufficient cold water to make a firm mixture. Roll out to line a 20-cm (8-in) flan case. Prick the bottom with a fork and cover with greaseproof paper. Fill with beans or lentils to weight down the pastry, then bake in the oven for 15 minutes. This is known as baking 'blind'. Remove from the oven, and take out lentils and greaseproof paper.

Clean and de-gut the mackerel, and poach in a little water until cooked – about 15 minutes depending on the size of the fish.

Wash the spinach thoroughly under running water. Put a knob of butter in a pan and add the spinach. Cover tightly and cook on a very low heat for about 10 minutes, shaking the pan from time to time to avoid sticking. When cooked, drain and press spinach between two plates to extract as much moisture as possible. Sprinkle grated nutmeg over it, then spread in the bottom of the flan case. Flake the fish and spread over the top. (If using canned mackerel drain excess oil from the can before using.)

Heat in a warm oven, 160°C (325°F)/Gas 3, for 20 minutes. Heat the grill, sprinkle grated cheese over the flan and brown under the grill before serving, taking care not to burn the pastry.

Haddock with Bacon Crisp

The strong taste of the crispy bacon pieces in this dish blends deliciously with the smoked haddock.

450 g (1 lb) smoked haddock
25 g (1 oz) butter
3 rashers streaky bacon
1 225-g (8-oz) can tomatoes
seasoning

Preheat oven to 180°C (350°F)/Gas 4. Grease a shallow ovenproof dish. Cut the fish into 5-cm (2-in) cubes. Trim rind and gristle from bacon and cut each rasher into three or four pieces. Put the haddock in the bottom of the dish. Scatter bacon over the haddock and then pour the tomatoes on top. Season well. Cover and cook in the oven for 30 minutes. Remove lid and allow bacon to crisp under the grill just before serving.

Spiced Whiting

You'll never guess it's the homely whiting when served this way.

4 medium-sized whiting
3 chillies or ¼ teaspoon chilli powder
3 pieces root ginger
6 cloves
¼ teaspoon each of turmeric, nutmeg and cinnamon
2 tablespoons sweet chutney
250 ml (¼ pint) water
25 g (1 oz) butter
25 g (1 oz) flour

Clean the fish and wipe them dry. De-seed chillies and chop into slices. Put the fish in a baking tin. Blend together all the other ingredients except the butter and flour and pour over fish. Cover and cook at 190°C (375°F)/Gas 5 for 30 minutes. Drain fish, retaining the liquid, and keep fish hot.

Melt the butter in a saucepan, remove from heat and stir in the flour, then the liquid in which the fish has been cooked. Return to the heat and stir until sauce has thickened. Pour over the fish and serve with boiled rice.

Liver Sweet'n'sour

450 g (1 lb) lamb's liver
4 rashers streaky bacon
450 g (1 lb) cooking apples such as Bramleys
2 medium-sized onions
2 tablespoons oil
seasoning
50 g (2 oz) raisins
250 ml ($\frac{1}{2}$ pint) beef stock

Slice the liver, trim rind and gristle from bacon and cut each rasher into three pieces. Peel, core and slice the apples, chop the onion.

Heat the oil in a pan and fry onion until soft. Remove and put into a casserole. Fry liver and bacon briefly on both sides. Cover the bottom of the casserole with liver slices, put half the bacon pieces on top of the liver, then cover with apple slices. Be sure to season each layer. Repeat, ending with the apples. Scatter raisins over the top, then pour in the beef stock. Cover and cook in a moderate oven, 180°C (350°F)/Gas 4, for 45 minutes.

Liver in Sour Cream

2 medium-sized onions
2 tablespoons vegetable oil
450 g (1 lb) pig's liver
25 g (1 oz) flour
salt
pepper
1 125-ml ($\frac{1}{4}$-pint) carton sour cream
125 ml ($\frac{1}{4}$ pint) stock

Preheat oven to 180°C (350°F)/Gas 4. Chop the onions finely and fry them in oil until soft but not brown. Cut pig's liver into slices and roll in the seasoned flour. Remove onions from oil, draining well and put them in bottom of a casserole. Fry liver until brown on both sides, then put the slices on top on the onions in the casserole. Blend sour cream and stock, and pour over the liver. Cover and cook for one hour.

Indian Kidneys

Tea gives a surprisingly rich flavour to this dish.

8 lamb's kidneys
2 medium-sized onions
4 rashers streaky bacon
2 tablespoons vegetable oil

25 g (1 oz) flour
250 ml (½ pint) cold tea
100 g (4 oz) mushrooms
salt
pepper
2 tablespoons top of milk

Put the kidneys in a pan of cold water, bring to a boil, then drain immediately and rinse. Peel and slice the onions. Trim rind and gristle from bacon and chop each rasher into four pieces. Heat the oil and fry onions until soft. Add bacon and fry until fat is transparent. Slice the kidneys and roll them in flour, then add them to pan with the tea and coarsely chopped mushrooms. Season well. Cover the pan and simmer for 15 minutes. Stir in top of milk, then reheat but do not boil. Adjust seasoning and serve with boiled rice.

Bacon Jambalaya

900-g (2-lb) bacon joint such as hock
25 g (1 oz) butter
2 medium-sized onions
225 g (8 oz) long grain rice
1 400-g (14-oz) can tomatoes
1 tablespoon tomato ketchup
375 ml (¾ pint) water
25 g (1 oz) grated cheese
chopped parsley
8 prawns to garnish

Cook the bacon joint by covering it with cold water and bringing slowly to the boil. Allow 25 minutes per pound and 15 minutes over. Drain and allow to cool.

Melt the butter in a deep saucepan. Chop the onions and fry them in butter until soft but not brown. Add rice, stirring well to prevent sticking. Add the canned tomatoes and ketchup, blending them thoroughly with the rice. Chop bacon into small dice and add to the pan. Gradually add the water throughout cooking as the rice absorbs the liquid. Stir frequently.

When the rice is cooked pile into a serving dish, sprinkle with grated cheese and brown under grill. Just before serving scatter with chopped parsley and garnish with whole prawns.

Spiced Spare-rib Chops

25 g (1 oz) flour
salt

pepper
2 tablespoons vegetable oil
4 spare-rib pork chops
4 tablespoons marmalade
2 tablespoons water
1 tablespoon cider vinegar
1 teaspoon caraway seed
1 teaspoon mustard powder

Preheat oven to 200°C (400°F)/Gas 6. Mix the flour and seasoning together. Heat the oil in a pan. Coat each chop with the seasoned flour, then fry meat on both sides until just brown. Put the chops in a shallow ovenproof dish. Mix marmalade, water, cider vinegar and the seasonings together. Pour the sauce over the chops, then bake for one hour.

Desserts

Tea Sorbet

The unexpected flavour of this sorbet will intrigue your guests. The choice of tea is of paramount importance, and it's really worth experimenting to chance on one that suits your particular taste. I use Twining's Nectar tea which is available fairly widely.

12.5 g (½ oz) good quality tea
500 ml (1 pint) water
150 g (6 oz) caster sugar
2 large lemons
1 egg white

Set the freezer compartment of your refrigerator to its coldest setting. Infuse the tea for five minutes in freshly boiling water. Strain through a very fine sieve or muslin and dissolve the sugar in the tea. Warm the lemons before cutting them (this will help to extract all the juice possible), then add lemon juice to the tea. Freeze. When mushy, remove and fold the stiffly beaten egg white into mixture. Refreeze.

This sorbet doesn't take as long to soften as most, so only take it out of the freezer compartment an hour before serving. It looks nice in glasses topped with a sprig of mint.

Banana Ice Cream

4 ripe bananas
125 ml (¼ pint) double cream
250 ml (½ pint) thick custard
½ teaspoon nutmeg

Turn the freezer compartment of your refrigerator to its coldest setting. Mash the bananas thoroughly and whip the cream until stiff. Blend bananas, cream, custard and nutmeg together in a blender if you have one or, failing that, beat until blended using a wooden spoon.

Turn into a plastic container, cover and freeze until firm. Remove from freezer, leave until mushy, then beat again. Refreeze. Put into the lower part of a refrigerator two or three hours before serving.

Ginger Rhubarb Fool

This is a light and flavourful dessert to serve after a heavy main meal. It is quite liquid in texture and should be served in wine glasses, with teaspoons.

450 g (1 lb) rhubarb
50 g (2 oz) root ginger (or 2 teaspoons ground ginger)
50 g (2 oz) brown sugar
1 125-ml (5-oz) carton natural yoghurt

Trim rhubarb and cut into 2.5-cm (1-in) pieces. If you are using root ginger, tie it up in a piece of muslin. Put the rhubarb with the ginger (root or ground) into a saucepan with 2 tablespoons water. Add sugar and simmer very gently until the rhubarb is soft. Remove root ginger and squeeze muslin to extract as much ginger flavour as possible.

Blend to a purée in a liquidiser or by pressing the mixture through a sieve with the back of a wooden spoon. When cool add the yoghurt and stir in well. Spoon into wine glasses and chill until ready to serve.

Apple Rhubarb Whip

225 g (8 oz) rhubarb
225 g (8 oz) apples after peeling and coring
2 tablespoons honey
250 ml (½ pint) thick custard
12 ratafia biscuits or gingernuts

Cut the rhubarb into 2.5-cm (1-in) pieces. Chop the apples and mix them into the rhubarb. Add honey. Add 2 tablespoons water and simmer over a low heat until fruit is soft. Sieve and add to custard, blending well together. If you have a blender, mix the fruit with the custard in that. Pour into four glasses and chill. Add ratafia biscuits just before serving or use gingernuts instead.

Rhubarb Banana Meringue

675 g (1½ lb) forced rhubarb
450 g (1 lb) ripe bananas
juice of ½ lemon
50 g (2 oz) sugar

For the meringue:
2 standard egg whites
100 g (4 oz) caster sugar

Trim the rhubarb and cut it into 2.5-cm (1-in) pieces. Mash the bananas with a fork and sprinkle them with lemon juice.

Into the bottom of an ovenproof dish put a layer of rhubarb and sprinkle with half the sugar. Spread banana on top, then a further layer of rhubarb. Sprinkle with the rest of the sugar.

To make the meringue, whisk the egg whites until stiff, then add one-third of the sugar. Whisk until the mixture will make peaks again, then add half the remaining sugar. Whisk until mixture looks 'satiny' in appearance. Fold in the remaining sugar with a metal spoon, just sufficiently to mix it in. Pour over the top of the rhubarb, so that the fruit is sealed in.

Bake at 160°C (325°F)/Gas 3 for 25–30 minutes.

Cinnamon Apples

675 g (1½ lb) cooking apples
3 tablespoons sugar
50 g (2 oz) butter
2 teaspoons cinnamon
100 g (4 oz) bread, grated into crumbs

Peel and core the apples and cut them into slices. Simmer in a little water with 2 tablespoons of the sugar until soft, then beat into a smooth purée using a wooden spoon. Leave to cool.

Melt the butter in a pan, stir in cinnamon, then add breadcrumbs and stir until crumbs have absorbed butter and spice. Stir in the remaining sugar.

For each serving put a layer of apple at the bottom of a wine glass, then a layer of the crumbs and continue to fill the glass, ending with a layer of apple.

Spiced Banana Flan

This is really delicious—and you'd better serve fairly small helpings as it is very rich.

50 g (2 oz) butter
1 level tablespoon golden syrup
150 g (6 oz) ginger biscuits
½ packet lemon jelly
2 tablespoons water
225 g (8 oz) cream cheese
1 small can full-cream condensed milk
2 lemons
3 bananas
½ teaspoon ground cinnamon

To make the flan base, melt the butter in saucepan, add the golden syrup and stir until blended. Crush ginger biscuits to coarse crumbs. This is best done if biscuits are put into a plastic bag and crushed with a rolling pin. Add the biscuits to syrup mixture and stir to mix. Press mixture around the outside of a fairly deep 17.5-cm (7-in) dish. It will adhere to the sides because of the syrup. Leave on one side.

To make the filling, melt the lemon jelly in 2 tablespoons water over a low heat. Whisk the cream cheese until light and fluffy, then blend in the jelly, condensed milk and juice of 1½ lemons. (Reserve the remaining half lemon for later.) More juice will be extracted from the lemons if they are left in hot water for a few minutes to soften them.

Mash 2 bananas, and spread them on the bottom of the flan dish. Sprinkle over the cinnamon, pour on the cream cheese mixture and leave to set for an hour or two.

Before serving, cut the remaining banana into thin slices (if you cut diagonally, rather than straight across, the slices look more attractive). Dip each slice in the lemon juice from the remaining lemon to prevent them browning, then arrange in lines over the top of the flan.

If you're feeling particularly sinful, serve with cream!

Pear Custard Tart

50 g (2 oz) butter
2 rounded tablespoons golden syrup
1 198-g (7-oz) packet ginger biscuits
125 ml (¼ pint) double cream
250 ml (½ pint) thick cold custard
2 pears
apricot jam for glaze

Melt the butter in a saucepan and stir in the golden syrup until blended. Crush ginger biscuits. This is easy to do if you place the biscuits in a plastic bag and use a rolling pin to crush them. Stir the crumbs into the syrup mixture and, when thoroughly mixed, use to line the edges of a 17.5-cm (7-in) flan dish, pressing the mixture well around the sides.

Whip the double cream and mix into the cold custard. Pour into the centre of the flan dish and chill.

Peel, core and slice each pear into four pieces. Unless they are very ripe, poach them in a little sugar and water until cooked. Arrange in the centre of the custard.

Melt 1 tablespoon apricot jam with 1 tablespoon water and brush over the pears as a glaze.

Grape Tart

For the hazelnut pastry:
25 g (1 oz) hazelnuts
150 g (6 oz) wholemeal flour
75 g (3 oz) butter
1 teaspoon brown sugar

For the filling:
3 tablespoons redcurrant jelly
100 g (4 oz) green grapes
100 g (4 oz) black grapes

For the garnish (optional):
two or three grapes of each colour
little egg white
caster sugar

Grill the hazelnuts and remove their outer skins by rubbing them with a cloth. Chop very finely.

Sieve the flour and rub in the butter until the mixture resembles fine breadcrumbs. Add hazelnuts, brown sugar, and enough water to make a firm dough. Line a 17.5-cm (7-in) loose-bottomed flan case, prick base with a fork and cook for 20 minutes at 190°C (375°F)/Gas 5. Remove from oven and immediately brush 2 tablespoons of the redcurrant jelly over the bottom of the pastry. Cut grapes in half and de-seed but do not skin them. Arrange the green and black grapes in alternate wedges over the flan case. Reserve two or three grapes of each colour. Heat remaining redcurrant jelly with 1 tablespoon of water and brush over the flan. Leave to cool. In the meantime, paint egg white over the remaining grapes and dip in caster sugar. Leave on a wire rack to dry. Just before serving, pile the frosted grapes in the centre of the flan.

Spiced Rhubarb Tart

If you are using forced rhubarb this amount of sugar is just right. If your rhubarb comes straight from the garden, add extra sweetening.

For the pastry:
150 g (6 oz) plain flour
75 g (3 oz) butter
1 tablespoon caster sugar

For the filling:
450 g (1 lb) rhubarb
25 g (1 oz) flour
50 g (2 oz) caster sugar
½ teaspoon ground cinnamon
1 125-ml (¼-pint) carton natural yoghurt

Preheat oven to 200°C (400°F)/Gas 6. To make the pastry, sieve flour and rub in butter until the mixture resembles fine breadcrumbs. Add sugar, then enough water to make a firm dough. Line a 17.5-cm (7-in) flan case with the pastry.

Top and tail rhubarb and cut into 2.5-cm (1-in) pieces. Put in the base of the flan. Mix flour with sugar and cinnamon, stir in yoghurt and pour over the rhubarb. Bake for 30 minutes.

Almond Cheesecake

For the rich shortcrust pastry:
250 g (8 oz) plain flour
125 g (4 oz) butter
25 g (1 oz) caster sugar
1 egg yolk
½ teaspoon salt
cold water to mix

For the filling:
1 225-g (8-oz) carton cottage cheese
75 g (3 oz) butter
75 g (3 oz) caster sugar
50 g (2 oz) ground almonds
50 g (2 oz) semolina
rind and juice of 1 lemon
2 standard eggs
egg white left from pastry
50 g (2 oz) raisins

Preheat oven to 180°C (350°F)/Gas 4. To make the pastry, sift flour and salt into a bowl. Cut butter into pieces and rub into flour until the mixture resembles fine breadcrumbs. Add sugar, then egg yolk (reserve the white for the filling) and enough cold water to mix to form a firm dough. Roll out to line a 22.5-cm (9-in) flan case. Prick the base with a fork then weight down with greaseproof paper and lentils or beans. Bake 'blind' for 10 minutes.

Mix the cheese with the butter, sugar, almonds, semolina, rind and lemon juice and the 2 egg yolks. Beat with an electric whisk if you have one. Whisk the 3 egg whites until stiff then fold into the cheese mixture with the flour using a metal spoon. Sprinkle raisins in the bottom of the flan, pour the mixture over them and return flan to oven for about $\frac{3}{4}$ of an hour.

Marmalade Queen Pudding

375 ml ($\frac{3}{4}$ pint) milk
1 tablespoon marmalade
12.5 g ($\frac{1}{2}$ oz) butter
12.5 g ($\frac{1}{2}$ oz) sugar
75 g (3 oz) fresh white breadcrumbs
2 eggs
50 g (2 oz) sugar for meringue
extra marmalade to serve as a sauce

Preheat oven to 160°C (325°F)/Gas 3. Heat the milk with the marmalade, butter and sugar until hot but not boiling. Pour this liquid over breadcrumbs and leave for 20 minutes to allow the bread to swell. Separate the eggs, add the yolks to crumbs, pour into a greased ovenproof dish and stand in a baking tin of cold water. Cook until set—about 25–30 minutes and remove from oven. Turn down the oven to 150°C (300°F)/Gas 2. Whisk the egg whites until stiff, fold in the sugar and pile over the crumb custard. Return to oven and cook for a further 20 minutes. The meringue should be firm to the touch but soft inside.

Serve at once with extra warmed marmalade as a sauce.

Baked Egg Custard

This is a beautifully light dessert that can be served plain or used with a variety of fruit purées served as a sauce. Or try black cherries, stewed and the juice thickened with a little arrowroot; black currants served in the same way make a pleasing contrast.

3 eggs
25 g (1 oz) sugar

500 ml (1 pint) milk
little grated nutmeg

Preheat oven to 160°C (325°F)/Gas 3. Break the eggs into a bowl and add sugar. Beat until whites and yolks are sufficiently blended. Warm the milk, then stir into the eggs. Leave until bubbles subside. Butter a deep pie dish, then strain in the milk and egg mixture using a fine sieve. Grate a little nutmeg over the top. Half fill a baking tin with cold water, and stand the pie dish in the middle. Bake for about 30 minutes or until the custard is firm to the touch.

Chocolate Coffee Cream

100 g (4 oz) plain chocolate
2 tablespoons instant coffee
¼ teaspoon vanilla essence
250 ml (½ pint) water
12.5 cm (½ oz) gelatine
125 ml (¼ pint) double cream
1 tablespoon rum (optional)
4 ratafia biscuits

Break chocolate into small pieces and place in a bowl with the coffee powder, vanilla essence, and 250 ml (½ pint) boiling water. Put 3 tablespoons cold water in a cup, then sprinkle over gelatine and heat gently until gelatine has melted. Pour into chocolate mixture, stir well and leave until it is beginning to thicken. At this point whip the cream, and add it to the chocolate mixture, together with the rum. Stir just enough to blend the ingredients. Spoon mixture into 4 small wine or sherry glasses and leave to set. Top each glass with a ratafia biscuit.

Apple Rice Condé

This looks very pretty served in a glass so that the layers show through.

450 g (1 lb) cooking apples
50 g (2 oz) round grain rice
500 ml (1 pint) milk
50 g (2 oz) caster sugar
½ teaspoon vanilla essence
1 egg

To garnish:
mint leaves or angelica

Cut the apples into pieces, but do not peel or core. Put them with 1 tablespoon water in a covered saucepan. Cook over a low heat until soft, shaking the pan from time to time to prevent sticking. When cooked, sieve or put through a Mouli if you have one. Leave to cool, then chill.

Put the rice in a saucepan with a little of the milk and cook for a few minutes to soften the grains. Add remaining milk, sugar and vanilla essence. Cook over a very gentle heat—use an asbestos mat if necessary—until rice is thick and creamy. Allow to cool.

Separate the egg. Add the yolk to the cooled rice and stir to blend. Whisk the egg white until stiff, then fold into the rice.

In six wine glasses put a layer of apple purée, then rice, and continue alternating, ending with a layer of rice. Chill until ready to serve, then garnish with mint leaves or angelica and serve at once.
Serves 6

Yoghurt Foam

Oranges and yoghurt combine beautifully to make this fresh-to-the-palate dessert. If you have a sweet tooth, add a little more sugar than stated.

2 large oranges
2 125-ml (¼-pint) cartons natural yoghurt
25 g (1 oz) caster sugar
1 125-ml (¼-pint) carton double cream
2 egg whites
angelica to decorate

Peel the oranges, removing white pith, and cut them into segments. Retain four segments and chop up the rest into rough pieces.

Mix yoghurt, caster sugar, orange pieces, and cream, thoroughly whipped. Whisk the egg whites until stiff and add to yoghurt, folding in only enough to blend. Divide into four serving dishes and arrange a slice of orange over the top, adding diamonds of angelica.

Orange Condé

This can be done in two stages—cook and chill the rice on one day and prepare the oranges the next. Serve really cold for maximum effect.

For the rice:
50 g (2 oz) round grain rice
500 ml (1 pint) milk
1 medium-sized orange
50 g (2 oz) caster sugar
1 rounded teaspoon gelatine
1 125-ml (5-oz) carton single cream

For the orange topping:
50 g (2 oz) caster sugar
125 ml (¼ pint) water
3 oranges

Put the rice with a little of the milk in a saucepan and bring to the boil to soften the grains. Grate the rind from the orange and put it at the bottom of an ovenproof dish, then add the softened rice, all the milk and the sugar. Stir, then cook in a very slow oven, 150°C (300°F)/Gas 2, for 2–2½ hours. Stir from time to time. The rice should be very creamy when cooked, so don't hurry it. Remove any skin that has formed, and allow to cool.

Extract the juice from the orange, put it in a cup and sprinkle in the teaspoon of gelatine. Stand the cup in a saucepan of water and heat until the gelatine has melted in the orange juice. Pour into the rice and stir gently, then add the cream. Transfer to a serving dish and leave to set. Chill if possible.

For the topping, put the sugar in a thick-based pan and allow it to colour slowly over a gentle heat. When the sugar is brown, add the water and stir. The mixture will spit at this stage. Stir and bring to a boil. Remove from heat. Peel the oranges, taking care to remove all the white pith, and cut into fairly thick slices. Soak in the caramel mixture and chill if possible.

Just before serving, put the orange slices in an overlapping ring over the rice mixture and pour over any remaining juice.

Gingerbread Banana Cake

Try to make the gingerbread a couple of days in advance. The flavours will develop if it is wrapped in foil or kept in a tin with a good tight-fitting lid.

150 g (6 oz) plain flour
¼ teaspoon salt
½ teaspoon bicarbonate of soda
2 teaspoons ground ginger
100 g (4 oz) black treacle
25 g (1 oz) lard
25 g (1 oz) soft brown sugar
1 large egg
2 tablespoons boiling water

For the filling:
1 125-ml (¼-pint) carton double cream
25 g (1 oz) caster sugar
2 ripe bananas
juice of ½ lemon

Sift flour, salt, bicarbonate of soda and ginger into a bowl. Put treacle, lard and sugar into a saucepan and heat gently until the lard has melted, the sugar dissolved and the liquid is tepid. Pour into the flour and mix with a wooden spoon. Add the beaten egg and finally 2 tablespoons boiling water.

Well grease and line a 17.5-cm (7-in) cake tin and pour in the mixture. Smooth over the top, then cook just below centre of the oven at 180°C (350°F)/Gas 4 for about an hour. Leave in the tin to cool, then wrap in foil and keep for a couple of days before using if possible.

To make up the cake, cut the gingerbread into two equal rounds. Whip the cream and fold in the sugar. Cut bananas in diagonal slices and dip in lemon juice to prevent discoloration. Mix half the bananas with half the cream and sandwich the two rounds together. Spread remaining cream on top and arrange the rest of the banana slices around the edge.

Orange Gingerbread

Use the same recipe as above but substitute oranges for bananas. Take three oranges and cut two into segments to mix with half the cream, retaining any juice to moisten the cake. Peel and cut remaining orange into rounds and use these to decorate the top of the cake.

SUMMER

The maddening thing about summer is that when there is such a marvellous array of fresh food available, unaccountably, we don't feel like cooking any more. The sun beckons enticingly and we linger over cool drinks, then suddenly there's a meal to prepare for a hungry family in five minutes flat. Fortunately the outstanding array of vegetables and fruits we have in this short season can be prepared simply to make exquisitely tempting dishes. Almost any vegetable can be served on its own as a first course.

The recipes here are mostly easy and quick to prepare and can be cooked on top of the stove. Flans, galantines and pâtés can be made in advance and carried on picnics, or eaten at home in the garden. With a crisp, brightly coloured salad to accompany, these dishes make some of the best summer meals in the world. Don't forget to take some French dressing separately; it's easy to carry in a screw-top bottle and can be added to the salad at the last minute. If the weather is really hot go for the no-cook sweets such as summer pudding or water ice.

Summer is also the time to be adventurous and try using fruit with meat. So many people are wary of this delicious combination and they just don't know what they're missing—try the Honeyed Chicken with Peaches and you'll see what I mean.

If the evenings turn cool, you can return to casseroles using cooked meat or minced beef to save on the cooking time. Serve them with a colourful salad to save even more cooking time, and if you're very hungry and still want something extra, serve French bread as well.

Starters

Green Pea Soup

500 ml (1 pint) chicken stock
450 g (1 lb) shelled green peas
sprig mint
seasoning
250 ml (½ pint) milk

Pour the chicken stock into a saucepan and add the shelled green peas, sprig of mint and seasoning. Bring to a boil and simmer gently for about 10–15 minutes until the peas are tender. If you have a blender, liquidise peas and stock in that. If not, rub peas through a sieve, being careful to retain all the liquid.

Just before serving add the milk. Heat slowly and re-season as necessary. Serve chilled or hot with a small sprig of mint floating on top.
Serves 5–6

Chilled Watercress Soup

A favourite classic summer soup. I prefer it thoroughly chilled but you can of course serve it hot.

225 g (8 oz) potatoes
1 medium-sized onion
25 g (1 oz) butter
1 bunch watercress
500 ml (1 pint) chicken stock
seasoning
125 ml ($\frac{1}{4}$ pint) milk

Peel the potatoes and cut them into thin slices. Chop the onion finely. Melt the butter in a saucepan and add the onion and potato. Cook very gently to soften onion but do not allow it to brown. Chop the watercress, removing any yellowing leaves, and add it to the potato and onion. Pour in the stock, season well, bring to a boil and allow to simmer for about 20 minutes.

If you have a liquidiser, purée the soup; otherwise press the mixture through a sieve using the back of a wooden spoon. Add milk and stir to blend. Adjust seasoning and allow the soup to chill very thoroughly before serving. If it is not chilled by the time you need it, add an ice cube to each soup bowl before serving.

Pea Pod Soup

It doesn't sound promising, but do try this unusually flavoured soup— which is unbelievably economical to make. Use only the peas at the beginning of the season when the pods are green and tender.

pods from 1 kg (2$\frac{1}{4}$ lb) shelled peas
1 medium-sized onion
3 sprigs mint
salt and pepper
approx 250 ml ($\frac{1}{2}$ pint) milk

A blender is really necessary for this soup. Wash the pea pods well, then put them in a pan with 1 litre (2 pints) water, the sliced onion and sprigs of mint. Simmer gently with the lid on until the pods are soft—about 2½ hours.

Blend in a liquidiser *and* put the purée through a sieve. This is because the pea pods are stringy at this stage. Season well with salt and pepper. To every two portions of soup add one of milk and reheat, adjusting seasoning.

Serve with hot buttered croûtons.

Lettuce Soup

A good way to use up too many lettuces from your garden. Or buy them when they are cheap at your local market.

225 g (8 oz) lettuce leaves
1 small onion
25 g (1 oz) butter
375 ml (¾ pint) chicken stock
black pepper
salt
250 ml (½ pint) milk
1 tablespoon top of the milk or cream
grating of nutmeg

Wash the lettuce leaves thoroughly and plunge them into boiling water. Simmer for 3 or 4 minutes, then drain and run under the cold tap. Chop the lettuce into shreds. Chop the onion finely, then fry it gently in the melted butter until soft but not brown. Add the shredded lettuce and stock to the pan, season with salt and pepper, bring to the boil and simmer for five minutes.

Liquidise or press through a sieve. Add the milk, adjust seasoning and reheat slowly. Just before serving, add the thin cream and a generous grating of nutmeg. Serve this soup piping hot.

Iced Cucumber Soup

If a liquidiser isn't available you can grate the cucumber and blend it with the other ingredients.

1 large cucumber
250 ml (½ pint) natural yoghurt
125 ml (¼ pint) milk
2 tablespoons white wine vinegar
salt and pepper
chopped mint

Wipe the cucumber and cut into small dice. Put into the liquidiser the cucumber, yoghurt, milk, vinegar and seasoning. You may have to do this in two stages depending on the size of your blender. Blend for a few seconds, then turn into a bowl and chill very well. If you don't have a liquidiser, finely grate the cucumber, combine with all the other ingredients and stir well before chilling. When serving the soup sprinkle a little chopped mint on top just before taking it to the table.

Tomato Salad

Undoubtedly one of the nicest and certainly one of the easiest starters to serve. Make sure the tomatoes are firm—freshly picked if possible.

4–6 large firm tomatoes
5 or 6 spring onions
French dressing (made with two parts oil to one part vinegar, salt, pepper, pinch sugar and mustard)

Slice the tomatoes thinly, and cut the spring onions into thin rings. Arrange the tomatoes in a shallow bowl, and scatter the onions over them. Season well, then spoon over the French dressing and serve immediately.

Green Brean Salad

Cold green beans, freshly cooked can be served in the same way, with onion and French dressing spooned over just before serving.

Spinach with Croûtons

Uncooked spinach is really good. Marinate it in a French dressing for an hour or so before serving, and add the croûtons just before you take it to the table.

450 g (1 lb) fresh spinach
2 tablespoons oil
1 tablespoon vinegar
salt
pepper
mustard
pinch sugar
2 thick slices bread
50 g butter
1 tablespoon Parmesan cheese (optional)

Wash the spinach really thoroughly and remove stalks. Dry carefully on kitchen paper or a clean tea towel. Chop the spinach roughly. Make the

French dressing by combining the oil, vinegar, seasoning, mustard and sugar, and pour over the spinach, tossing it lightly as you would a salad. Leave for at least an hour.

To make the croûtons cut the crusts off the bread (use day-old bread, not too fresh) and cut into small cubes. Melt the butter in a pan and when foaming add bread cubes. Fry quickly, turning them in the butter so they are evenly coated. Sprinkle over the spinach just before serving. A tablespoon of Parmesan cheese can be added if you wish.

Stuffed Courgettes

This is a delicious starter to a summer meal, but I often make it for lunch if I have the oven going for something else. If you serve if for lunch, try it with garlic bread.

8 medium-sized courgettes
1 large or 2 medium-sized onions
2 tablespoons vegetable oil
2 cloves garlic
4 tablespoons tomato purée
seasoning
100 g (4 oz) grated Cheddar cheese

Preheat the oven to 190°C (375°F)/Gas 5. Cut each courgette in half lengthwise. Carefully cut out the centres, leaving enough in the shells so that they will hold their shape during cooking. Blanch the shells in boiling water for 2 minutes, then drain. Chop the onions finely, and fry them gently in hot oil until soft. Chop the garlic or use a garlic press if you have one. Add the scooped out flesh from the courgettes, the garlic and tomato purée to the pan. Season well.

Put the courgettes in a shallow baking tin and fill each one with some of the mixture. Sprinkle generously with grated cheese and bake at the top of the oven for 35 minutes.

Mushroom and Cottage Cheese Cocotte

4 eggs
125 ml (¼ pint) warm milk
50 g (2 oz) white finely grated breadcrumbs
100 g (4 oz) mushrooms
1 225-g (8-oz) carton cottage cheese
mustard
salt and pepper
little lemon juice or milk

Beat the eggs with a wooden spoon until the whites are blended. Pour the warm milk over the breadcrumbs and allow the crumbs to swell. Chop the mushrooms, but retain about six to slice as a garnish.

Combine the egg, breadcrumbs, chopped mushrooms and cheese. Season well. Pour the mixture into individual cocotte dishes or one flameproof dish. Stand dish or dishes in a baking tin with cold water about halfway up. Cook at 180°C (350°F)/Gas 4 for 7–10 minutes if you are using cocotte dishes, or 25–30 minutes if you are using one large dish.

Slice the remaining mushrooms and dip the slices in a little lemon juice or, if you prefer, poach them in a little milk and arrange as a garnish on top before serving.

Spinach in Cheese Sauce

This makes a tasty starter to a meal, but you can serve it on toast to make a light supper or luncheon dish.

1 kg (2¼ lb) spinach
knob butter
25 g (1 oz) butter
25 g (1 oz) flour
250 ml (½ pint) milk
100 g (4 oz) grated cheese
grated nutmeg

Wash the spinach very well indeed under a running tap. Shake dry. Put a knob of butter in a saucepan with a close-fitting lid. Add the spinach and heat over a very low flame, shaking frequently until the spinach has reduced and is cooked.

To make the sauce, melt 25 g (1 oz) butter in a pan, remove from heat and stir in the flour. Gradually add the milk, return the pan to the heat and stir until thickened. Add 75 g (3 oz) of the grated cheese and beat to blend.

Press the spinach between two plates to extract as much moisture as possible. This may sound rather a lot of trouble but it is the best way of extracting excess moisture. Grate nutmeg over the spinach, then divide into four small fireproof dishes. Pour the cheese sauce over the spinach. Sprinkle the remaining grated cheese on top and brown under a hot grill until cheese is bubbling.

Liver Sausage Spread

This is a spread rather than a pâté and can be served simply, with thin toast, as a starter. To make it more elaborate, pile the spread on a bed of lettuce and surround it with tomato rings.

225 g (8 oz) liver sausage
100 g (4 oz) cream cheese
1 small onion, grated
2–3 tablespoons mayonnaise
2 tablespoons chopped thyme
sage and parsley mixed

Put all the ingredients into a bowl and beat them hard with a wooden spoon until blended. Leave to chill and thicken slightly before serving.

Avocado Mousse

A versatile mixture, this mousse can be served as a cocktail dip with savoury biscuits. Presented in little pots and accompanied by brown bread and butter it makes a good starter to a special meal. Or, by adding 250 ml (½ pint) milk or chicken stock you can turn it into an excellent chilled soup.

Buy avocados when they are at their cheapest—for these recipes it won't matter if they are slightly over-ripe.

2 avocado pears
1 large lemon
125 ml (¼ pint) double cream
salt and pepper
slivers of lemon to garnish

Cut the avocados in half and remove the stones. Scoop out all the flesh and blend it with a fork, then add the juice of one lemon, mixing well so that a smooth consistency is obtained. Season with salt and pepper. Gradually stir in cream, chill and serve in one of the ways described above.

Minted Grape Ring

A refreshing and tangy start to a summer meal.

½ packet lemon jelly
100 g (4 oz) black grapes
1 tablespoon chopped mint
lettuce leaves to garnish

Make the jelly with 250 ml (½ pint) water according to the instructions on the packet. Put a thin layer of jelly in a 17.5-cm (7-in) ring mould. Peel and de-seed the grapes. The easiest way to do this is to peel them, cut them in half lengthwise, and then take the seeds out. Place the halved grapes, cut side up, around the bottom of the ring mould. Leave to set. Put another layer of jelly in the ring and sprinkle some of the chopped mint over it. Continue with alternate layers of grapes and jelly, ending with a layer of jelly.

Turn out on to a bed of lettuce and serve with thinly cut brown bread and butter.

Summer Surprise

2 bunches watercress
1 125-ml ($\frac{1}{4}$-pint) carton natural yoghurt
25 g (1 oz) almonds
paprika pepper

Trim the watercress and chop it coarsely. Pour over the yoghurt and stir to blend. Chop the almonds finely—easiest if you use a wet knife—then brown them under the grill.

Divide the cress between four plates and sprinkle the almonds on top. Add a dusting of paprika pepper and serve with fingers of toast.

Salmon Condé

A very good recipe for making a little salmon go a long way.

225 g (8 oz) cooked fresh salmon
1 green pepper
3 tablespoons French dressing (2 tablespoons oil, 1 tablespoon white wine vinegar, seasoning, pinch mustard and sugar)
100 g (4 oz) cooked rice
4 medium-sized hard tomatoes
2 tablespoons mayonnaise
4 lettuce leaves
1 tablespoon chopped parsley

Remove skin and bones from salmon and flake into small pieces. De-seed the pepper, chop into slices and blanch in boiling water for 2–3 minutes. Drain. Make up the French dressing and pour it over the cooked rice, stirring until it is thoroughly mixed. Peel the tomatoes by nicking their skins and then dipping them for a minute into boiling water. They will then peel easily. Chop the tomatoes and the pepper into small pieces and add to the rice. Mix the salmon with the mayonnaise.

Wash the lettuce leaves and dry them on a cloth or kitchen paper. Put one on each plate, then divide rice evenly between the plates. Spoon the salmon mixture on top of the rice and sprinkle with a generous amount of chopped parsley.

Main Courses

Pork Chops with Apple Cider

2 tablespoons vegetable oil
4 pork chops
2 medium-sized onions
salt and pepper
2 cooking apples
250 ml ($\frac{1}{2}$ pint) cider
50 g (2 oz) mushrooms

Heat the oil in a frying pan and fry the chops on both sides. Remove and put into a deep ovenproof casserole. Peel and finely chop the onions, then cook them in the oil until soft and golden. Add the onion to the casserole with the chops, and season well. Peel, core and thickly slice the apples and place on top of chops. Pour in the cider.

Cover and cook in a preheated oven, 180°C (350°F)/Gas 4, for 1 hour. Remove from oven, add the sliced mushrooms and return to cook for a further 20 minutes.

Rosemary Lamb with Forcemeat

Try to use fresh rosemary if you can. This recipe gives a plain joint of roast lamb a new flavour, and is well complimented by new potatoes and fresh spinach.

$\frac{1}{2}$ leg of lamb
100 g (4 oz) pork sausage meat
2 slices white bread (grated)
seasoning
large sprigs of fresh rosemary or 2–3 tablespoons dried rosemary
50 g (2 oz) cooking fat
1 tablespoon flour
1 teaspoon cinnamon

Bone the leg of lamb or ask the butcher to do it for you. Mix the sausage meat with the breadcrumbs, seasoning and chopped rosemary. Press this mixture into the cavity left by the bone and reshape the joint, tying with string as necessary. Preheat oven to 190°C (375°F)/Gas 5. Put the fat in a roasting tin and heat in the oven.

Blend the flour and cinnamon together and rub over the joint of meat, pressing in well. Stand the meat in the roasting tin, and add any remaining rosemary. Roast in the oven for 1$\frac{1}{2}$ hours, basting occasionally.

Summer Lamb Casserole

This is an excellent way to use up lamb if you've cooked an overlarge joint.

450 g (1 lb) cooked lamb
450 g (1 lb) carrots
450 g (1 lb) courgettes
seasoning

For the sauce:
25 g (1 oz) butter
25 g (1 oz) flour
250 ml ($\frac{1}{2}$ pint) milk

For the topping:
50 g (2 oz) grated cheese
50 g (2 oz) crushed branflakes

Preheat oven to 180°C (350°F)/Gas 4. Cut the lamb into bite-sized pieces. Slice the carrots thinly. Top and tail courgettes and cut into thin rings. Into an ovenproof casserole put layers of lamb, carrots and courgettes. Season between each layer.

To make the white sauce, melt the butter in a pan, take off the heat and stir in the flour. Add milk gradually, stirring to keep the sauce smooth. Return to heat and stir until sauce has thickened. Pour over the ingredients in the casserole, then cover and place in the oven for 45 minutes.

Remove lid, scatter the grated cheese mixed with the branflakes on top and brown under a hot grill.

Lamb Curry

1 kg (2$\frac{1}{4}$ lb) leg of lamb
1 tablespoon vegetable oil
25 g (1 oz) butter
25 g (1 oz) chopped fresh ginger
2 cloves garlic
2 large onions
2 tablespoons curry powder
2 tablespoons tomato purée
1 tablespoon peanut butter
1 bay leaf
salt and pepper
1 teaspoon each of coriander seed, turmeric and cumin
2 tablespoons desiccated coconut soaked in 125 ml ($\frac{1}{4}$ pint) hot milk
250 ml ($\frac{1}{2}$ pint) chicken stock

Bone the leg of lamb and cut it into 5-cm (2-in) pieces. Melt the butter and oil in a deep saucepan and fry the meat until brown on all sides. Remove meat. Chop the ginger finely and fry together with the chopped garlic and sliced onions. Add the curry powder, tomato purée, peanut butter, bay leaf, seasoning and spices and stir with a wooden spoon to prevent them sticking. Then add coconut, chicken stock and finally the meat.

Cover and simmer over a very gentle heat for about 2 hours or until tender. Long slow cooking is necessary to allow the flavours to develop. Curries also benefit from being cooked one day and served the next.

Beef Layer Pie

A deliciously simple casserole which takes a little more time than normal to prepare. The smell of the cooking, however, makes it well worth while, and that's before you've tasted a mouthful!

450 g (1 lb) stewing beef
2 tablespoons vegetable oil
salt and pepper
1 bay leaf
250 ml (½ pint) beef stock
2 medium-sized onions
450 g (1 lb) potatoes

For the sauce:
25 g (1 oz) butter
25 g (1 oz) flour
125 ml (¼ pint) meat stock
75 g (3 oz) grated cheese

Cut the beef into 2.5-cm (1-in) cubes. Heat 1 tablespoon oil in a pan and fry meat until brown on both sides. Season with salt and pepper. Add the bay leaf and 250 ml (½ pint) stock, bring to a boil and simmer for 1 hour.

Chop the onions and fry them slowly in the remaining tablespoon of oil until soft. Peel the potatoes and slice them very thinly.

Drain the meat, retaining the liquid. Put a layer of meat at bottom of a greased ovenproof casserole, add a layer of onions, then a layer of potatoes. Season well. Continue layering meat, onion and potato, ending with a potato layer.

To make the sauce, melt the butter in a saucepan, remove from heat, stir in the flour then gradually add 125 ml (¼ pint) of the meat stock. Return to heat and stir until thickened, then mix in 50 g (2 oz) of the grated cheese. Pour the sauce over meat, cover the casserole and cook for 1½ hours at 180°C (350°F)/Gas 4. Remove from the oven, take off lid and sprinkle with remaining cheese, then brown under the grill.

Minced Beef Loaf

This is really quick to make and perfect to serve to unexpected guests.

450 g (1 lb) minced beef
100 g (4 oz) branflakes
1 225-g (8-oz) can tomatoes
salt
pepper
2 tablespoons chopped parsley
sage and thyme mixed
1 large egg

Mix together all the ingredients except the egg. Stir to distribute herbs and seasoning evenly. Beat the egg in a basin, then add to the meat.

Preheat the oven to 190°C (375°F)/Gas 5. Line a 1-kg (2-lb) loaf tin and press the mixture in firmly. Cover with greaseproof paper and stand the tin in a baking tray of cold water. Place in the middle of the oven and cook for $1\frac{1}{4}$ hours. Serve hot or cold.
Serves 6

Beef in Apple Cider

The addition of the apples and apricots makes a small amount of beef go a long way.

100 g (4 oz) dried apricots
225 g (8 oz) cooking apples
1 medium-sized onion
1 tablespoon vegetable oil
675 g (1½ lb) topside beef
4 tablespoons cider
1 tablespoon brown sugar
250 ml (½ pint) beef stock
salt and pepper

Soak apricots in water for 3–4 hours. Peel, core, and slice the apples and chop the onions finely. Heat the oil and sear the meat on all sides, then transfer it to a large casserole with the rest of the ingredients. Cook for 2 hours in a moderate oven, 180°C (350°F)/Gas Mark 4. Serve the meat in slices with the sauce spooned over the top.

Country Garden Beef

This is a homely family supper made to look special by the colourful addition of carrots and courgettes.

48

225 g (8 oz) carrots
3 or 4 medium-sized courgettes
1 large onion
450 g (1 lb) minced beef
seasoning
1 198-g (7-oz) can tomatoes

Slice the carrots thinly. Top and tail the courgettes, slice them and finely chop the onion.

Into an ovenproof casserole put layers of the minced beef, carrots, chopped onion and courgettes, seasoning well between each layer. Finally pour in the canned tomatoes, mashing the pulp with a fork to make it more liquid. Cover and cook the casserole for one hour at 180°C (350°F)/Gas 4.

Chicken Galantine

Most attractive to look at, this galantine is a perfect choice for a light summer supper. The tarragon gives it a unique flavour.

1 1.35-kg (3-lb) chicken
seasoning
½ cucumber
6 good sprigs tarragon
100 g (4 oz) ham
12.5 g (½ oz) gelatine

Put the chicken into a large saucepan, cover with water, add seasoning. Bring to a boil and simmer gently for 1 hour, or until the chicken has cooked. Drain and allow to cool, but retain 375 ml (¾ pint) of the chicken stock. Remove meat from the carcass and chop into fairly small pieces. Slice the cucumber into very thin, transparent rings—use a mandolin if you have one. At the bottom and also around the sides of a 1-kg (2-lb) loaf tin arrange the cucumber rings. Take half the tarragon sprigs and arrange decoratively alongside the cucumber. Chop remaining tarragon finely. Pack a layer of chicken over the cucumber, pressing down firmly. Sprinkle with tarragon, then add chopped ham, and season well. Add more chicken and tarragon and season again.

Measure out 375 ml (¾ pint) stock. Pour 2–3 tablespoons of the stock in a cup, and sprinkle in the gelatine. Heat by standing the cup in a pan of simmering water until the gelatine has melted. Add to the rest of the stock, stir and pour over chicken. Leave to set.

To turn out, dip the tin in a bowl of hot water, then invert it on to a plate. Cut with a sharp knife when serving.

Chicken with Mushrooms

This is just the right dish to serve on a cold summer evening. It is light but served hot.

450 g (1 lb) cooked chicken
75 g (3 oz) butter
50 g (2 oz) flour
250 ml (½ pint) chicken stock
salt and pepper
100 g (4 oz) mushrooms
2 tablespoons cream

Flake the chicken meat into small pieces. Melt 50 g (2 oz) of the butter in a pan, remove from the heat and stir in flour. Add the chicken stock slowly, then heat, stirring continually, until the sauce has thickened. Add the chicken meat, season well and continue to heat slowly for 5–10 minutes. Chop the mushrooms. Melt the remaining butter in a pan and fry the mushrooms for a few minutes. Add them to chicken, and just before serving add the cream. Adjust seasoning and serve at once.

Chicken with Grapes

The French call this Poulet Veronique. Don't let the grapes overcook or they will disintegrate.

4 pieces frying chicken
½ lemon
50 g (2 oz) butter
125 ml (¼ pint) white wine
1 bay leaf
black pepper and salt
100 g (4 oz) mushrooms
100 g (4 oz) green grapes
1 tablespoon cream

Wipe the chicken and sprinkle the juice of half a lemon over the pieces. Melt the butter in pan and fry the chicken until brown on both sides. Add the wine, seasoning and sliced mushrooms. Cover tightly and simmer for 30–35 minutes until the joints are cooked. Halve the grapes and remove any pips. Add the grapes to the chicken and cook for 3–4 minutes more. Remove chicken and grapes and keep hot. Add 1 tablespoon cream to the liquid, reheat, and pour over chicken before serving.

Honeyed Chicken with Peaches

Even people who claim they don't like the combination of meat and fruit will fall for this delicately flavoured dish.

4 large chicken joints
25 g (1 oz) melted butter
2 tablespoons clear honey
2 tablespoons cider vinegar
1 teaspoon mustard powder
4 medium-sized ripe peaches
salt and pepper

Preheat oven to 190°C (375°F)/Gas 5. Wipe the chicken joints and brush them all over with the melted butter. Put them in a baking tin. Blend together honey, cider vinegar and mustard and spoon the mixture over the joints. Dust with salt and pepper. Bake in the moderate oven for 35–40 minutes.

While the chicken is baking, skin the peaches by dipping them into boiling water for a minute or two. The skin will then come off easily. Cut peaches in half and remove stones. Add to the chicken dish, baste with the juices in the pan and continue cooking for a further 20 minutes. Serve with boiled rice and brightly coloured vegetables such as new carrots and garden peas.

Chicken Breasts in Mayonnaise

4 chicken breasts
250 ml (½ pint) cider
small sprig sage (or 1 teaspoon dried sage)
salt and pepper
2 cloves garlic
4 tablespoons mayonnaise
2 hard-boiled eggs
12 black olives
2 tomatoes

Poach the chicken breasts in the cider with the sage and seasoning until cooked—about 25 minutes. Allow to cool in the liquid, then drain. Crush the cloves of garlic or use a garlic press if you have one. Blend with the mayonnaise. Arrange chicken on a serving dish. Carefully spoon the mayonnaise over each chicken joint. Slice the hard-boiled eggs into quarters and arrange them round the chicken. Cut each olive in half and add to chicken, and finally place the thinly-sliced tomatoes around the edge of the dish.

Veal with Mackerel Sauce

The flavours of meat and fish blend well, and mackerel adds spice to the innocuous veal. For this recipe, canned mackerel gives a stronger flavour.

4 veal escallops
bunch spring onions
1 198-g (7-oz) can mackerel
250 ml (½ pint) chicken stock
seasoning
2 medium-sized tomatoes
1 tablespoon cream or top of the milk

Preheat oven to 190°C (375°F)/Gas 5. Beat escallops with a rolling pin and put them in a shallow casserole. Cut up the spring onions and sprinkle over the top of the veal. Drain oil from can of mackerel, then flake the fish and put on top of the veal. Pour the stock into the casserole and season well. Slice the tomatoes and arrange over the top. Cover and cook in the oven for 1 hour. Strain off the sauce and boil rapidly until it thickens. Add 1 tablespoon cream or top of milk. Reheat carefully, pour over the veal and serve.

Kidneys Jerez

8 lamb's kidneys
2 level tablespoons flour
pinch nutmeg
½ level teaspoon salt and pepper
25 g (1 oz) butter
125 ml (¼ pint) beef stock
8 stuffed green olives
chopped parsley

Put the skinned kidneys into cold water, bring to the boil, drain and rinse. Core and slice the kidneys. Combine flour, nutmeg and seasoning and coat kidneys thoroughly. Heat butter in a frying pan and cook the kidneys, including all the flour, for about 8 minutes. Add the stock, stirring until blended and thickened. Cook for a further five minutes. Add halved olives, and serve on a bed of plain boiled rice sprinkled with parsley.

Summer Fish Plate

450 g (1 lb) fresh haddock
salt
pepper
25 g (1 oz) butter
25 g (1 oz) flour

125 ml (¼ pint) milk
125 ml (¼ pint) mayonnaise
small bunch spring onions
4 tomatoes
½ cucumber
2 medium-sized carrots (grated)
1 tablespoon chopped parsley

Cook the haddock gently in a little water, drain and flake. Season well.
Make a white sauce by melting the butter in a pan, removing from the heat
and stirring in the flour. When the flour is well mixed add the milk, a little
at a time, stirring constantly to keep the sauce smooth. Return pan to the
heat, and stir some more. When the white sauce has thickened, remove
from heat, cool, then whisk in mayonnaise and blend with the flaked fish.
Chop the spring onions and add to mixture. Arrange in the centre of large
plate, then cut the tomatoes into thin rings and arrange them around the
fish. Slice the cucumber very thinly and arrange around tomatoes. Finely
edge with the grated carrot. Chop parsley very finely, sprinkle over fish and
serve.

Smoked Haddock Mousse

This smoked fish dish with just a hint of curry is perfect served cold on a
hot day, for lunch or a light supper, but you could use it as a dinner party
starter for six at any time of year.

450 g (1 lb) smoked haddock
125 ml (¼ pint) milk and 125 ml (¼ pint) water mixed
black pepper
bay leaf
25 g (1 oz) butter
25 g (1 oz) flour
1 teaspoon curry powder
1 lemon
1 12.5-g (½-oz) packet gelatine
1 125-ml (5-oz) carton sour cream
2 eggs
bunch watercress

Put the haddock in a saucepan with the milk and water, black pepper and
bay leaf. Simmer for about 10 minutes, then drain, retaining liquid.
Remove bones and skin, and flake the fish. Rinse out pan. Melt the butter
and remove pan from heat. Stir in the flour and curry powder, then add the
fish stock slowly, return the pan to the heat and stir until the sauce is thick.
Add flaked fish.

Squeeze the juice of one lemon into a cup and sprinkle gelatine over. Heat over a pan of water until gelatine has melted. Add to fish and stir well. Add sour cream. Break the eggs into a bowl and whisk them over hot water until they are thick and creamy. Fold into fish. Pour the mousse mixture into a greased 17.5-cm (7-in) ring mould and leave to set. Just before serving turn out and decorate with watercress in the centre. Serve with thinly cut brown bread and butter.

Mackerel with Gooseberries

The tartness of the gooseberries offsets the somewhat oily taste of mackerel.

4 mackerel
675 g (1½ lb) gooseberries
75 g (3 oz) sugar
150 g (6 oz) breadcrumbs
salt and pepper
1 tablespoon vegetable oil

Clean and gut the mackerel. Top and tail the gooseberries. Put them in a pan, add the sugar (more or less than called for above depending on the ripeness of the gooseberries) and a little water. Bring to a boil and simmer for 2–3 minutes. Mix four tablespoons gooseberries with breadcrumbs, add seasoning and a little of the gooseberry juice to moisten. Fill the cavity of each mackerel with stuffing. Brush fish with oil and grill for 5 minutes on each side. Purée the remaining gooseberries to make a sauce, and serve this separately.

Fish with Chutney Sauce

This is a really easy recipe—it's very tasty but calls for a minimum of effort.

675 g (1½ lb) white fish (coley is cheapest)
1 standard egg
2 tablespoons milk
seasoning
2 tablespoons mild chutney
2 tablespoons branflakes

Preheat oven to 190°C (375°F)/Gas 5. Cut the fish into four equal pieces and put them into a shallow ovenproof casserole. Combine the beaten egg and milk and pour this over the fish. Spread the chutney on top, season well and finally sprinkle with the branflakes.

Cover and cook in the oven for 25–30 minutes.

Country-Style Pâté

A delicious pâté, just right to be eaten out of doors, in your own garden or on picnics.

250 ml (¼ pint) milk
bay leaf
1 small onion
325 g (12 oz) pig liver
225 g (8 oz) sausage meat or skinless pork sausages
7 rashers streaky bacon
25 g (1 oz) butter
25 g (1 oz) flour
salt
pepper
1 tablespoon chopped sage and thyme mixed (or 1 tablespoon sage and onion stuffing mix)

Pour the milk into a pan together with the bay leaf and the onion, cut in half. Heat slowly, and when nearly boiling remove from the heat and allow milk to absorb the flavour of the onion and bayleaf.

Chop the liver into small pieces and cut up the sausages. Take 3 streaky bacon rashers, remove rind and gristle and chop finely. Put all this through a mincer. If you have a blender place these three ingredients in the blender and leave while you prepare the sauce.

Melt the butter, remove from heat and stir in flour. Add the strained milk, stirring all the time until smooth, then return the pan to the heat and stir briskly until sauce thickens.

If you have minced the meat, add it to the sauce with the chopped herbs or stuffing and season well. If you are using a blender pour the sauce and herbs over the meat and switch on at full speed until blended thoroughly.

Line a 1-kg (2-lb) loaf tin with greaseproof paper. Trim the remaining bacon rashers and line the base and sides of the tin with these. Pour in the liver mixture and cover with buttered greaseproof paper.

Fill a baking tin with 2.5 cm (1 in) cold water, put the loaf tin in the middle and bake in centre of oven, 160°C (325°F)/Gas 3 for 2 hours. Remove from oven and immediately press two weights on top and keep them there until the pâté has completely cooled.

Cider Rabbit with Raisins

The lovely smell of rabbit cooking gently in cider makes it well worth while cooking this dish alone. The cider gives a really good flavour too.

675 g (1½ lb) rabbit joints
25 g (1 oz) flour

3 rashers streaky bacon
12 baby onions
2 tablespoons vegetable oil
bay leaf
salt and pepper
500 ml (1 pint) cider
100 g (4 oz) raisins

Wipe the rabbit joints and coat them in flour. Trim rind and gristle from bacon and cut each rasher into three pieces. Peel the onions. Heat the oil in a frying pan and fry the streaky bacon. Add the rabbit and onions. When the rabbit is just brown and the onions have been coated in the oil, add the bay leaf, salt and pepper, and cider. Cover with a tight-fitting lid and simmer gently for one hour. Add the raisins and cook for a further hour.

Summer Sausage Flan

If you prepare the flan case ahead of time, this dish can be made very quickly. It tastes good hot or cold, so it's a good choice for your picnic basket.

150 g (6 oz) wholemeal flour
½ teaspoon salt
75 g (3 oz) butter
1 standard egg

For the filling:
1 medium-sized onion
225 g (8 oz) courgettes
100 g (4 oz) mushrooms
25 g (1 oz) butter
salt and pepper
4 cooked pork sausages

Sift the flour and salt into a bowl and rub in the butter with your fingertips until the mixture resembles fine breadcrumbs. Add the beaten egg and enough water to mix to a stiff dough. Roll out to line a 17.5-cm (7-in) flan case. Prick the bottom with a fork and cover with greaseproof paper. Fill with beans or lentils to weight down the pastry and bake 'blind' in a 190°C (375°F)/Gas 5 oven for 15 minutes. Remove lentils and greaseproof paper and allow to cool.

Chop the onion finely, top and tail the courgettes and slice them into 2.5-cm (1-in) pieces. Slice the mushrooms. Melt the butter in a pan and fry the onion until soft but not brown, then add the courgettes. Continue cooking gently for a further 5 minutes. Add the mushrooms and just coat them in the juices.

Season the vegetables to your taste, then pile them into the flan case. Cut each sausage in half lengthwise and place the pieces, flat side down, in a wheel shape on top of the courgette mixture. Cover the flan with foil and cook for 20 minutes at 180°C (350°F)/Gas 4.

Red Peppers with Rice and Kidney Stuffing

This is an attractive looking supper dish. For really hearty appetites serve two peppers per person and double all the ingredients.

4 large red peppers
250 g (8 oz) long grain rice
8 lamb's kidneys
2 rashers bacon
1 165-g (6-oz) can tomatoes
salt and pepper
1 teaspoon Soy sauce

Cut 'lids' off the tops of the red peppers and remove the seeds. Bring a pan of water to the boil and blanch the whole peppers with their lids, for 2 or 3 minutes. Remove from water, drain, and put on one side. Put the rice into boiling salted water and cook for 12 minutes, stirring from time to time to prevent sticking. Drain the rice into a sieve and run cold water through it to remove the starch. Leave to cool. Put the kidneys into a saucepan of cold water and bring to the boil slowly. As soon as it has boiled, discard water and rinse kidneys very thoroughly and cut into pieces. Cut the bacon into small pieces and fry with the kidneys until cooked. Mix with the rice. Add the tomatoes from the can, but retain the juice. Mix in well, adding salt and pepper and Soy sauce.

Fill each pepper with the rice mixture, then replace the top. Put into an ovenproof dish and pour over the tomato liquid from the can. Cover with foil, then put into the oven, 190°C (375°F)/Gas 5 and bake for 30 minutes.

Ratatouille Flan

The walnut pastry really does give this flan an added 'kick', but of course you can use plain white flour if you wish.

For the pastry:
150 g (6 oz) wholemeal flour
½ teaspoon salt
75 g (3 oz) butter
25 g (1 oz) finely chopped walnuts
1 egg
water to mix

For the filling:
1 medium-sized onion
25 g (1 oz) vegetable oil
2 cloves garlic
1 aubergine
1 large green pepper
1 375-g (13-oz) can tomatoes
350 g (12 oz) courgettes
100 g (4 oz) mushrooms
seasoning

Sift together the flour and salt into a bowl. Rub in the butter until the consistency resembles fine breadcrumbs. Mix in the walnuts, then add the beaten egg to the dry ingredients with sufficient cold water to make a firm mixture. Roll out to line a 17.5-cm (7-in) flan case. Prick the bottom of the flan and line it with greaseproof paper filled with lentils. Cook for 15 minutes at 190°C (375°F)/Gas 5. This is known as baking 'blind'. Remove lentils and allow to cool.

To make the ratatouille filling, chop the onion finely, and gently fry it in hot oil until soft but not coloured. Add the 2 cloves of garlic, cut up finely or crushed with a garlic press. Peel and slice the aubergine and add to the pan. Stir from time to time with a wooden spoon. Slice the pepper into rings discarding stalk and pips, and add to the mixture. When the pepper is slightly softened add tomatoes (with their liquid) and the thinly sliced courgettes. Season well. Put a close-fitting lid on the pan and allow mixture to cook gently for about 10 minutes. Add sliced mushrooms and cook for a further 5 minutes. Drain away any surplus liquid. Pile into the flan case and put back into the oven for a further 10–15 minutes.

Savoury Cheese Pudding

1 225-g (8-oz) carton cottage cheese
100 g (4 oz) ham
1 tablespoon mayonnaise
2 stalks chopped celery
1 small onion (grated)
3–4 slices buttered bread with crusts removed
seasoning
1 teaspoon mustard
1 egg
250 ml (½ pint) milk
2 tomatoes

Mix together cottage cheese, chopped ham and mayonnaise. Add the chopped celery and grated onion. Put a piece of bread and butter in the bottom of an ovenproof dish and spread with some of the mixture. Add salt, pepper and mustard. Add another slice of bread and more mixture, and so on, ending with a slice of bread, buttered side up. Beat the egg in a basin, add milk, then pour over dish. Slice the tomatoes and arrange the pieces around the edge. Bake in a moderate oven, 180°C (350°F)/Gas 4 for 25 minutes.

Mushroom and Yoghurt Flan

Bake the pastry case in advance and you can assemble this delicious summer flan in no time at all. The wholemeal flour definitely tastes better than ordinary flour, so do try to find some.

150 g (6 oz) wholemeal flour
½ teaspoon salt
75 g (3 oz) butter

For the filling:
100 g (4 oz) mushrooms
1 125-ml (¼-pint) carton natural yoghurt
bunch spring onions
salt and pepper
½ cucumber
sprigs of watercress

Sift the flour and salt into a bowl and rub in the butter with your fingertips until the mixture resembles fine breadcrumbs. Add enough water to mix to a stiff dough. Roll out to line a 17.5-cm (7-in) flan tin and prick the base with a fork. Bake at 190°C (375°F)/Gas 5 for 20–25 minutes. Leave to cool.

Chop the mushrooms into coarse pieces, and stir in the yoghurt. Cut the spring onions into small pieces and add to the mixture. Season well, and pile into the cooled flan case. Cut the cucumber into very fine transparent rings and edge pastry with these. Put a few sprigs of watercress in the centre and serve cold.

Desserts

Gooseberry Ice Cream (1)

This ice cream is rather beige in colour, but I hesitate to suggest adding green colouring as it so often turns out strident. It is made without sugar, but if you have a sweet tooth add 50 g (2 oz) sugar to fruit when cooking.

1 small can evaporated milk
500 ml (1 pint) thick gooseberry purée (approx 750 g (1½ lb) gooseberries)
green colouring (optional)

Boil unopened can of evaporated milk in a pan of water for 15 minutes. Cool, then chill in a refrigerator for 2–3 hours.

Turn the freezer compartment of the refrigerator to its coldest setting. Top and tail gooseberries. Put them in a pan with 250 ml (½ pint) water and simmer gently until soft. Press through a nylon sieve, using the back of the wooden spoon to force the mixture through. If necessary, make up to 500 ml (1 pint) with water. Leave to cool.

Whisk evaporated milk until thick and creamy. This takes time, but the mixture should at least double in bulk. Add gooseberry purée, blend together and add a few drops of green colouring if you wish. Pour into ice trays or a plastic container and freeze for 3–4 hours. Before serving put ice cream into ordinary part of refrigerator for about an hour. If you have stored it in a deep freeze, leave in fridge for 2–3 hours before serving.

Gooseberry Ice Cream (2)

Here's another version, and of course most fruit purées can be substituted for gooseberry. The custard and cream gives this ice cream a velvety texture.

450 g (1 lb) gooseberries
3 tablespoons water
2 tablespoons caster sugar
1 level tablespoon custard powder
250 ml (½ pint) milk
1 egg
65 ml (2½ fl oz) double cream

Turn the freezer compartment of your refrigerator to its coldest setting. Top and tail the gooseberries and put them with the water and half the caster sugar in a saucepan. Cook gently until soft. Press through a sieve and leave the purée to cool. Make the custard with the remaining sugar and the milk in the usual way. Leave to cool with a piece of wet greaseproof paper over the top to prevent a skin forming. Separate the egg and beat the yolk into the cooled custard. Add the gooseberry purée. Whisk the cream until stiff, then fold into the mixture. Finally, whisk the egg white until stiff and fold that in.

Pour into a container and put in the freezer compartment. Leave until 'slushy'. Whisk again, then put it back into a (500-ml) 1-pint pudding basin and freeze until hard. Leave inverted on a plate to thaw for serving and cut in wedges.

Peach Sorbet

This is one of the most refreshing sorbets I know, and perfect for a hot summer evening.

6 small ripe peaches
50 g (2 oz) caster sugar
whites of 2 standard eggs

Set the freezer compartment of your refrigerator to its coldest setting. Dip the ripe peaches in boiling water for 2 or 3 minutes and then take off the skins. Cut the flesh in to smallish pieces and either liquidise them or rub them through a nylon sieve.

Beat the caster sugar into the purée and pour into a freezer tray. Freeze for about two hours until mushy, then whisk again. Fold in the stiffly beaten egg whites, pour back into the freezer tray and refreeze.

Serve with sponge finger biscuits. I like them with ginger snaps too, but you might feel it destroys the delicate flavour of the sorbet.

Pineapple Water Ice

This is a very nice sweet to serve, as it's refreshing after a heavy main course and looks really great when served in the pineapple shells and topped with sprigs of mint.

325 g (12 oz) pineapple pulp (from either two small pineapples or one big one)
rind and juice of 1 lemon
150 g (6 oz) sugar
375 ml (¾ pint) water
1 egg white
a few sprigs mint

Turn the freezer compartment of your refrigerator to its coldest setting. Split pineapple in two down the entire length. Cut out the flesh and retain the shells. Cut the flesh into small pieces taking care to retain as much of the juice as possible.

Put the sugar and water into a saucepan and heat slowly until the sugar has dissolved. Add the lemon rind, which has been finely pared, leaving the white pith behind. When the sugar has dissolved, boil rapidly for five minutes. Remove from heat, add the juice of the lemon and pour liquid over the pineapple pulp. Cool, then place in the icemaking compartment of the refrigerator for several hours. When the mixture is 'mushy', remove and beat briskly. Whisk the white of 1 egg until stiff, then fold into the pulp, stir just enough to blend. Put back into the freezer compartment of the refrigerator and leave until frozen. Remove to the main part of the refrigerator about an hour before serving. Pile into the pineapple shells and decorate with small sprigs of mint just before taking it to the table.

Pineapple Supreme

This is a really spectacular sweet to serve to favourite guests. Wait until pineapples are cheap and make sure the ones you choose are really ripe.

2 small pineapples
2 peaches
225 g (8 oz) redcurrants
miniature bottle cointreau
mint leaves to garnish

Cut each pineapple in half lengthwise and carefully scoop out the flesh. Start cutting it with a knife and finish with a spoon so you can extract all the flesh without piercing the skin. Skin the peaches by dipping them for a minute or two in boiling water. Slice thinly, and remove the stones. Wash and pick over the redcurrants. Put all the fruit into a bowl and pour over the cointreau. Chill in a refrigerator for two or three hours.

Pile the fruit back into the pineapple shells, and finally garnish with mint leaves just before serving.

Peach and Almond Cream

Ripe juicy peaches are essential for this recipe. Make it up and serve it without allowing it to stand.

4 large ripe peaches
1 125-ml ($\frac{1}{4}$-pint) carton double cream
25 g (1 oz) caster sugar
$\frac{1}{4}$ teaspoon vanilla essence
12 ratafia biscuits
25 g (1 oz) almonds

Skin the peaches by dipping them in boiling water for a few minutes. The peel will then come off very easily. Halve each peach and remove the stones.

Whip the cream with the caster sugar and vanilla essence until it is fairly stiff. Crush ratafia biscuits until they are crumb-like, then fold them into the cream.

Chop almonds and toast them to a golden brown under the grill.

Put two peach halves on each plate and spoon cream on top; sprinkle over toasted almonds and serve at once.

Peaches in Spiced Red Wine

One of the most delicious desserts I have ever tasted was one I encountered in Cattolica, Italy, at the height of the tourist season. I had gone to look round a small family hotel and it was the proprietor's birthday. After all the hotel guests had had lunch, I was invited to join family and friends for their own celebratory meal.

Course followed course, and I was in grave danger of bursting there and then. Every time I wanted to refuse anything a fellow guest hissed, 'You must have some, otherwise they'll think it impolite.'

When I felt that anything else to eat would have the direst consequences along came this dessert—peaches in red wine. I took a reluctant sip, then another and another until the dish was empty. It is deliciously refreshing and remains a favourite of mine to this day.

8 small ripe peaches
250 ml (½ pint) red wine
2.5-cm (1-in) piece cinnamon stick
caster sugar

Skin the peaches by immersing them in boiling water for a minute or two. The skin will then be easily removed. Chop each peach into small slices. Heat the wine gently with the cinnamon, then allow wine to cool and remove cinnamon stick. Pour the wine over the peaches, sprinkle the top with caster sugar and chill thoroughly before serving.

Apricots can be used in the same way and taste just as good.

Apricots in Orange Sauce

Chill the fruit really well before serving as it brings out the delicious orange flavour.

450 g (1 lb) apricots
rind and juice of 1 orange
4 tablespoons clear honey
125 ml (¼ pint) water

Halve and stone the apricots. Put them in a saucepan together with the orange rind, which you have first pared thinly. Squeeze the juice from the orange and add to the pan with the honey and water. Poach the apricots in the liquid until cooked. The time will depend on the ripeness of the fruit, but it could take about 15 minutes. Turn into a dish, leave to cool, then chill thoroughly. Serve with cream.

Blackcurrant Kissel with Mint

If well chilled, this is extremely pleasant on its own. To make a more substantial sweet serve it with cinnamon toast.

450 g (1 lb) blackcurrants
4 tablespoons granulated sugar

500 ml (1 pint) water
2 teaspoons arrowroot
2 tablespoons chopped mint
2 or 3 teaspoons caster sugar

Wash and pick over the blackcurrants. Over a gentle heat, dissolve the sugar in the water, then add the blackcurrants. Bring to the boil and simmer for 2–3 minutes. Blend the arrowroot with some of the juice in the pan. Add to the rest of the blackcurrants and stir until it boils and thickens. Remove from heat and add the finely chopped mint. Sprinkle with two or three teaspoons caster sugar to prevent a skin forming and chill until very cold.

To make cinnamon toast, cut thinly sliced bread (with crusts removed) into fingers. Melt some butter in a pan, add a little demerara sugar and ground cinnamon and fry the bread in this. Drain and serve hot.

Redcurrant Delight

225 g (8 oz) cream cheese
1 125-ml (¼-pint) carton natural yoghurt
1 125-ml (¼-pint) carton soured cream
225 g (8 oz) redcurrants

Put the cream cheese through a fine sieve and blend in yoghurt and soured cream to mix well. If you have a blender, mix them together in that. Spoon into a shallow serving dish, smooth over the top with a knife and leave to chill. Just before serving, pile the washed and prepared redcurrants on top. You can if you wish sprinkle the redcurrants with caster sugar for a sweeter effect.

Macaroon Layer Dessert

8 macaroons
1 125-ml (¼-pint) carton double cream
caster sugar
225 g (8 oz) raspberries

Crumble the macaroons and whip the cream until stiff. Put a layer of macaroons in each of four glass dishes, cover with a layer of raspberries, and sprinkle with caster sugar. Add a layer of whipped cream. Repeat once, ending with a layer of cream.

Allow to stand for half an hour before serving so that the raspberry juice can penetrate the macaroon.

Gooseberry Ginger Layer

The addition of two heads of elder flowers when cooking the gooseberries adds most marvellously to the flavour of this dessert. It's well worth trying to find them.

250 ml (½ pint) thick gooseberry purée (from approx 450 g (1 lb) gooseberries)
250 ml (½ pint) thick custard
packet ginger biscuits
50 g (2 oz) butter

Beat the thick gooseberry purée into the custard. Crush the ginger biscuits with a rolling pin. This is easier if they are first placed in a plastic bag. Melt the butter, then stir in biscuit crumbs. Layer the gooseberry mixture and crumbs in tall wine glasses. End with a gooseberry layer. Chill well until ready to serve.
Serves 6 in wine glasses

Gooseberry Mousse

450 g (1 lb) gooseberries
3 eggs
75 g (3 oz) caster sugar
1 125-g (5-oz) carton double cream
12.5 g (½ oz) gelatine
25 g (1 oz) flaked almonds

Top and tail gooseberries and cook in about 125 ml (¼ pint) of water until soft. Put through a sieve to make a thick purée. If you have a blender use that to make the purée, but you must still sieve the gooseberries to eliminate the pips. Put aside to cool. Meanwhile, separate the yolks from the whites of egg, and whisk the yolks and the sugar over hot water until really thick and creamy in colour. Add the gooseberry purée and mix in. Dissolve the gelatine by putting two tablespoons water in a fireproof container and sprinkling the gelatine on top. Place in a small pan of hot water and heat slowly over the flame until the gelatine has dissolved. Stir the bottom to make sure it is evenly distributed, cool a little, then pour into the fruit mixture and mix in well. Whip the cream until it is the same thickness as the fruit mixture, then fold it in lightly. (If you wish to decorate the mousse with cream keep some in reserve. I prefer to use toasted almonds as the only decoration.) Whisk the egg whites until they are stiff and fold them in. Leave the mousse to set in a dish, preferably in a refrigerator. Flake almonds—it is easier if you use a wet sharp knife—then toast them gently under the grill, or leave them in a warm oven if you are using it at the time. Just before serving the mousse, sprinkle the almonds over the top.

If you feel particularly indulgent, serve more cream separately.

Gooseberries à la Creme

The natural green of gooseberries needs a little help with food colouring to become a delicate shade.

450 g (1 lb) gooseberries
125 ml ($\frac{1}{4}$ pint) water
75 g (3 oz) sugar
2 teaspoons gelatine
2 tablespoons water
125 ml ($\frac{1}{4}$ pint) double cream
1 egg white or 1 tablespoon top of milk
$\frac{1}{2}$ teaspoon green food colouring

To decorate:
few pieces of angelica
2 black grapes

Top and tail gooseberries, and put them in a saucepan with the water and sugar. Bring to a boil and simmer gently until the fruit is soft. Rub through a sieve. Put the water into a cup and sprinkle in the gelatine. Place the cup in a pan of hot water and heat gently until gelatine has thoroughly dissolved. Add to the gooseberry purée, and leave to cool. As the mixture is beginning to thicken, whip the cream and egg white or milk together until fairly stiff then fold into the purée. Add the green food colouring. Spoon into sundae dishes. Cut each black grape in half lengthwise and remove pips. Put in the centre of the sundae dish. Make diamond 'leaves' from angelica and put them at either side of the halved grapes. Chill until ready to serve.

Apricot Cream

450 g (1 lb) fresh apricots
4 tablespoons water
$\frac{1}{2}$ small brown loaf
50 g (2 oz) butter
2 tablespoons demerara sugar
$\frac{1}{2}$ teaspoon ground ginger
125 ml ($\frac{1}{4}$ pint) double cream
1 egg white
4 sprigs mint

66

Halve and stone apricots and poach them gently until soft in 4 tablespoons water. Drain off the juice and keep separately. Sieve the apricots to make a purée. Add a little of the juice, but keep the purée thick.

Remove crusts from bread and grate into crumbs. Melt the butter in a pan and when it is foaming add the sugar and ginger. Stir in the breadcrumbs and coat them with butter, then remove the pan from the heat. Whisk the double cream with the egg white until stiff. Add the apricot purée and stir until blended.

Into each of four sundae glasses spoon a layer of apricot cream, then a layer of crumbs (reserving some of them) and a further layer of apricots. Sprinkle a few breadcrumbs on top of each glass, in the centre. Chill until ready to serve then top with a sprig of mint.

Summer Pudding

Deceptively simple, this sweet is quite sumptuous when made carefully.

450 g (1 lb) mixture of fruit such as redcurrants, raspberries, blackcurrants etc
3 tablespoons granulated sugar
6–7 slices bread

Wash and pick over the fruit and put in a saucepan with 4 tablespoons water and the sugar. Bring to a boil and simmer gently until the fruit is soft. Leave to cool.

Use a (500-ml) 1-pint pudding basin, and carefully shape the bread to make an exact lining for the bowl. Start with the bottom shape, then, removing the crusts as you go, line all round the edge. Where there are gaps, fit in wedges of bread. Adjusting the sweetening if necessary, pour in half the fruit and juice, then add another slice of bread with crusts removed. Pour in the rest of the fruit and add the remaining bread to make a carefully fitting lid. Put a plate on top with a weight on it and leave overnight.

Turn out carefully, and serve with thick double cream.

Strawberry Apricot Gâteau

Because this is a fatless sponge cake it will not keep, so make it and eat it on the same day.

For the sponge:
3 standard eggs
75 g (3 oz) caster sugar
75 g (3 oz) flour

For the filling:
225 g (8 oz) strawberries
225 g (8 oz) apricots
50 g (2 oz) caster sugar
1 125-ml (¼-pint) carton double cream

To make the sponge, preheat the oven to 180°C (350°F)/Gas 4. Grease and line 2 17.5-cm (7-in) sandwich tins.

Break the eggs into a grease-free bowl. Whisk lightly until eggs and yolks are blended. Add sugar and whisk until thick and creamy. If you are doing this by hand, stand the basin over hot water, making sure the basin doesn't touch the water. If you use an electric whisk this isn't necessary. Whisk until the mixture will leave a trail. Fold in the flour with a metal spoon. Be gentle and blend it just enough to distribute the flour evenly. Pour at once into the sandwich tins and cook for about 20 minutes. Remove from the oven, and leave to cool for a minute or two before turning out on to a wire rack.

Hull and pick over the strawberries. Cut the apricots in half and remove the stones, then poach them in a very little water with sugar to taste until fairly soft. Drain and cool. Whisk cream until stiff and fold in the sugar. Take half the cream and stir into it the apricots and about one-third of the strawberries, chopped.

To assemble the cake, put one of the sponge cakes on a cake plate and spread over the apricot cream. Top with the other sponge cake. Spread over the remaining cream and arrange the strawberries around the edge of the cake.

Summer Fruit Gâteau

A really moist sponge that isn't easy to turn out of the tin. Take your time, but if you do make a mess of it, it can always be patched up with jam or cream.

For the sponge base:
3 large eggs
pinch salt
75 g (3 oz) caster sugar
75 g (3 oz) semolina
25 g (1 oz) ground almonds
1 teaspoon baking powder
25 g (1 oz) melted butter

For the filling:
75 g (3 oz) caster sugar
125 ml (¼ pint) water
2 peaches

68

225 g (8 oz) redcurrants
1 125-ml (5-fl oz) carton double cream
sprigs of mint

Preheat oven to 190°C (375°F)/Gas 5. Grease 2 17.5-cm (7-in) sandwich tins. To make the sponge, separate egg yolks from whites. Whisk the egg whites until stiff, then fold in the sugar and beat again until the mixture holds its shape. Gradually beat in the egg yolks. Fold in the semolina, ground almonds and baking powder. Lastly stir in the melted butter. Divide the mixture between the two greased sandwich tins and bake in the oven for 15 minutes or until the sponges shrink a little from the sides of the tins.

In the meantime, dissolve 50 g (2 oz) of the caster sugar in the water and poach the whole peaches until cooked. (If the peaches are very ripe you can omit this and just boil the sugar syrup on its own.) When the peaches are cooked spoon all the syrup over the two cooked sponges and leave in the tin until cool. Skin and slice the peaches.

To assemble the cake, wash, top and tail the redcurrants and sprinkle them with the remaining sugar. Whisk the cream until stiff.

Remove the sponges from the tins and place one on a cake plate. Cover with redcurrants and half the cream. Top with remaining sponge, and cover with cream. Arrange peach slices over the top and decorate with well-washed sprigs of mint.

Lemon Cheesecake

1 packet lemon jelly
2 tablespoons water
450 g (1 lb) curd cheese
2 125-ml (5-oz) cartons sour cream
2 lemons
150 g (6 oz) wheatmeal biscuits
50 g (2 oz) butter
lemon slices to garnish (optional)

Melt the lemon jelly with the 2 tablespoons water over a low heat. Whisk it into the curd cheese until well blended. Add the sour cream and the juice of 2 lemons. Continue whisking until smooth. Pour into a mould or medium shallow dish and smooth the top.

Crush the wheatmeal biscuits—easiest if they are put in a plastic bag first. Melt the butter, stir in the crumbs, then scatter the coated crumbs evenly over the top of the cheesecake, pressing them down very lightly. Leave to set, and just before serving decorate with paper-thin slices of lemon.
Serves 6–8

Gooseberry Mallow Flan

You'll love the gooey look of this flan. The marshmallows melt while you're serving it, so be careful with the cutting.

For the pastry:
150 g (6 oz) plain flour
pinch salt
75 g (3 oz) butter
1 teaspoon caster sugar
milk for brushing pastry

For the filling:
450 g (1 lb) gooseberries
50 g (2 oz) sugar
12 marshmallows

Make the pastry by sifting the flour and salt into a bowl. Rub in the butter until the mixture resembles fine breadcrumbs. Add the sugar and enough cold water to mix to a firm dough. Roll out to line a 17.5-cm (7-in) pastry case. Reserve pastry leftovers to make a lattice. Leave to chill in the fridge.

Preheat the oven to 190°C (375°F)/Gas 5.

Top and tail the gooseberries, and cook them with the sugar in 2 tablespoons water until soft. Purée by pressing through a nylon sieve using the back of a wooden spoon. Pour the purée into the pastry case and roll out the pastry trimmings to make a wide lattice. Seal the pastry edges together by moistening the edges with water. Brush pastry with milk and cook for 30 minutes. Remove from oven, place a marshmallow between each lattice diagonal, and serve immediately with cream.

AUTUMN

Autumn is a time of nature's over-indulgence when it comes to apples, pears, plums, nuts and hosts of other foods that seem to rain on us during the season. It's a mixed season, for summer is still smiling at us in the beginning and fruits such as home-grown apples and pears and plums are in abundance. Peaches are still cheap and plentiful, too. As the season progresses, carrots, parsnips and swedes come into full season and add variety to casseroles.

It's a time for using imagination if the never-ending stream of apples and pears are to pass the family jury without 'Oh, no, not that again'. Many of your garden windfalls can be used for making chutneys and jams, as apples, in particular, form an integral part of so many relishes. Apple purée keeps well in a refrigerator and can be used for pies and crumbles as well as the recipes in this chapter.

My family always eat the ripe pears before I've had a chance to use them in cooking, but they always leave me the windfalls and any which the birds or maggots have attended to first. There are usually a lot of these and for recipes like spiced pears uneven pieces can be used just as well as halved or quartered fruit.

Take the family on a blackberry outing if you possibly can. If the children are small take damp flannels, for the juice stains not only clothes but hands and faces too. Carry a good deep basket to put them in as well. Even now I remember a sortie I made as a schoolgirl to gather blackberries. I scurried across the road to dash for the homebound bus, only to drop the lot in its path. All that remained of my afternoon's work was a juicy stain in the road and a mottled red dress which my mother wasn't too pleased about.

Weather alternates between hot and cold in this season, but hot meals are generally the order of the day. At home we always seem to find that autumn is a time for trying new experiences—it's something to do with starting evening classes again I suspect—so you might be tempted to try the pigeon pie or grey mullet, or one of the spicy dishes with some savoury rice.

Starters

Mushroom Baked Eggs

100 g (4 oz) mushrooms
25 g (1 oz) butter
4 eggs
salt
pepper

Preheat oven to 160°C (325°F)/Gas 3. Clean and slice the mushrooms, and fry them for a few minutes in the melted butter. Butter four ramekin dishes and divide the mushrooms equally between them. Break an egg into each dish, season with salt and pepper. Stand the dishes in a baking tin and half fill tin with hot water. Bake for about 10 minutes in the centre of the oven. It's important that the eggs are fairly runny and not baked hard: the whites should be just set but no more. Serve with triangles of toast.

Egg Lyonnaise

4 eggs
225 g (½ lb) onions
25 g (1 oz) butter

For the sauce:
25 g (1 oz) butter
25 g (1 oz) flour
250 ml (½ pint) milk
100 g (4 oz) grated cheese

Hard boil the eggs and put them in cold water until ready to use. Chop the onions finely and fry them gently in melted butter until just browned. Drain well by piling them on to kitchen paper.

To make the cheese sauce melt the butter in a pan, remove from the heat and stir in the flour. Gradually add the milk and return the pan to the heat, stirring continuously until the sauce thickens. Add the onions and half the grated cheese.

Shell the hard-boiled eggs, cut them in half lengthwise and place the halves flat side down in a flameproof dish. Spoon over the sauce. Cover with buttered greaseproof paper and reheat in oven, 180°C (350°F)/Gas 4, for about 20 minutes. Remove paper, sprinkle remaining cheese on the top and brown under the grill. Serve at once.

Cream of Mushroom Soup

25 g (1 oz) butter
25 g (1 oz) flour
500 ml (1 pint) chicken stock
250 ml (½ pint) milk
100 g (4 oz) mushrooms
juice of ½ lemon
seasoning
2 tablespoons chopped parsley

Melt the butter in a pan, and remove from the heat. Stir in the flour, then gradually add chicken stock and milk. Return pan to heat and bring to a boil, stirring until the liquid has thickened. Chop the mushrooms very finely, add to the liquid together with the juice of half a lemon, and seasoning to taste. Simmer the mushrooms for 3–4 minutes. Sprinkle a little chopped parsley in the centre of each bowl of soup just before serving.

Bacon and Lentil Soup

Buy bacon pieces from the grocer as they are usually fairly cheap and give this soup a wonderful flavour.

100 g (4 oz) bacon pieces
1 medium-sized onion
50 g (2 oz) lentils well washed
750 ml (1½ pints) chicken stock
1 tablespoon chopped sage and thyme
seasoning

Trim rind from bacon pieces and chop fairly small. Fry gently to extract fat. Chop the onion, add to the bacon and fry in the fat. When the onion is soft, add the lentils, herbs and seasoning. (Bacon makes this fairly salty so be sparing with other seasoning.) Pour in the stock, bring to the boil, then cover and simmer for about an hour, stirring from time to time.

Put the soup through a sieve. Retain bacon pieces, chop very finely and put them back in the soup. Reheat and serve.

Almond Soup

100 g (4 oz) almonds
1 medium-sized onion
25 g (1 oz) butter
1 tablespoon chopped parsley
1 litre (2 pints) chicken stock

seasoning
250 ml (½ pint) milk
25 g (1 oz) cornflour
nutmeg

Pour boiling water over the almonds, leave a few minutes, then shell and chop them. Chop the onion finely. Melt the butter in a pan, add the almonds and onion and cook very gently to soften the onion, but do not allow it to brown. Add chopped parsley and the stock, and season well. Bring to the boil and simmer for 15–20 minutes. Liquidise in a blender if you have one, or press through a sieve using the back of a wooden spoon.

Take a little of the milk to blend the cornflour to a smooth paste. Add this, with the rest of the milk, to the soup and bring to the boil, stirring. Adjust seasoning and sprinkle with a grating of nutmeg before serving.

Iced Pear Soup

1 kg (2¼ lb) pears
500 ml (1 pint) water
vanilla pod or teaspoon vanilla essence
50 g (2 oz) sugar

Peel, core and slice pears into small pieces and put them in a saucepan with the water and vanilla pod or essence. Bring to a boil and simmer until pears are soft. Remove the vanilla pod, rub the soup through a sieve and add sugar, then leave to cool and chill very thoroughly. Serve with very thinly cut brown bread and butter.

Mushroom and Onion Flan

150 g (6 oz) plain flour
75 g (3 oz) butter
pinch salt
water to mix

For the filling:
bunch spring onions
225 g (8 oz) mushrooms
25 g (1 oz) butter
2 eggs
125 ml (¼ pint) milk
seasoning

Preheat oven to 190°C (375°F)/Gas 5. Sift flour and salt into a bowl and rub in the butter until the mixture resembles fine breadcrumbs. Mix with sufficient water to make a firm dough. Roll out to line a 17.5-cm (7-in) pastry case. Prick the bottom of the pastry case with a fork, and fill with greaseproof paper and beans or lentils. Bake for 10–15 minutes. This is known as baking 'blind'. Remove lentils and greaseproof paper.

Prepare spring onions and chop them into 2.5-cm (1-in) pieces. Slice the mushrooms. Melt the butter in a pan and gently fry the onions and mushrooms. Spread the mixture in the bottom of the flan. Beat the eggs together, add milk and seasoning. Pour over the flan and set in the oven for 15–20 minutes or until set.

Carrot and Cottage Cheese Flan

This flan is a pleasant starter to any meal, but by making two and serving half a flan as a single portion, you could use it as a supper dish.

For the hazelnut pastry:
150 g (6 oz) wholemeal flour
75 g (3 oz) butter
25 g (1 oz) hazelnuts

For the filling:
1 large egg
100 g (4 oz) cottage cheese
3 or 4 carrots
25 g (1 oz) butter
generous grating of nutmeg

Grill the hazelnuts and remove the outer skins by rubbing them with a cloth. Chop them very finely. Preheat the oven to 190°C (375°F)/Gas 5. Sieve flour and rub in butter until the mixture resembles fine breadcrumbs. Stir in the nuts, then add enough water to make a firm dough. Line a 17.5-cm (7-in) loose-bottomed flan case and prick the base with a fork. Cook for 10 minutes in the oven.

Break the egg into a bowl, then beat in the cottage cheese until well blended. Pour this into the flan case, and return to the oven to cook for a further 15 minutes or until the cheese has set.

In the meantime, slice the carrots very thinly—use a mandolin if you have one. Melt the butter in a pan, and cook the carrots over a very gentle heat, shaking the pan from time to time. When the flan has set, drain the carrot slices and arrange them, overlapping, on top of the flan. Sprinkle generously with nutmeg and return to oven to warm up if necessary.

Savoury Grapefruit

A very quick starter that is quite unusual.

2 grapefruit
1 large orange

1 red apple
3 or 4 leaves chicory
1 125-ml (¼-pint) carton natural yoghurt
1 teaspoon cinnamon

Cut each grapefruit in two, and take out the flesh with a sharp knife. Peel the orange and cut it into segments. Cut the apple into pieces, removing the core but retaining the skin. Dip the pieces into salted water to prevent browning. Cut the chicory leaves into small shreds. To assemble, drain the apple slices, put all the ingredients into a bowl and pour the yoghurt over them. Stir to blend. Spoon back into the grapefruit shells and just before serving sprinkle with cinnamon.

Savoury Nest Eggs

4 soft rolls
50 g (2 oz) butter
3 rashers streaky bacon
1 medium-sized onion
2 eggs
125 ml (¼ pint) milk
seasoning
four lettuce leaves
2 tomatoes

Scoop out the centre of the rolls, leaving a good shell remaining. Brush inside and outside with melted butter and bake in a moderate oven, 180°C (350°F)/Gas 4, for about 15 minutes.

In the meantime, melt remaining butter and fry chopped bacon and onion and grated crumbs from the hollowed out rolls. Add the beaten eggs mixed with the milk, season well, turn down the heat and scramble very slowly. Divide the mixture into four, pile into each roll and serve on a bed of lettuce garnished with tomatoes.

Celery in Almond Butter

2 heads celery
50 g (2 oz) almonds
100 g (4 oz) butter

Trim the celery and cut each head in half. Plunge into boiling salted water and simmer for five minutes. Remove and drain.

Chop the almonds well and brown either in the oven if you have it on, or gently under a grill. Melt the butter and add almonds.

Put the four celery halves into an ovenproof dish, then spoon over the almond butter. Cook at 180°C (350°F)/Gas 4 for 25 minutes.

Stuffed Aubergine

2 aubergines
2 medium-sized onions
2 cloves garlic
1 tablespoon cooking oil
1 tablespoon chopped sage and thyme
75 g (3 oz) cooked rice
100 g (4 oz) cooked chicken or lamb
1 185-gm (6½-oz) can tomatoes

Cut the aubergines in half lengthwise. Scoop out the flesh from the shells, using a spoon. Be careful to keep the shell intact. Finely chop the onion and the garlic.

Heat oil in a pan and fry the onion and garlic until soft, then add the aubergine pieces and chopped herbs. Continue frying until the aubergine is soft and nearly cooked. Add the cooked rice and meat, chopped into small pieces. Pile the mixture back into aubergine shells. Pour the canned tomatoes through a sieve and press them with a wooden spoon to obtain a thick purée. Put the aubergines in an ovenproof dish, pour over the tomato and cover with foil. Bake in the oven at 190°C (375°F)/Gas 5 for 30 minutes.

Autumn Salad

½ white cabbage about 350 g (12 oz)
50 g (2 oz) mushrooms
2 carrots
100 g (4 oz) cooked ham
50 g (2 oz) cooked green peas
2 tablespoons wine vinegar
6 tablespoons oil
pinch sugar and mustard
clove garlic
salt and pepper

Wash the cabbage and shred it finely, removing the centre stalk. Slice the mushrooms, grate the carrots and dice the ham. Mix all the vegetables and the ham together in a bowl. Make up the French dressing with the vinegar, oil, sugar, mustard, crushed garlic, salt and pepper. Pour this over the salad, and mix thoroughly. Leave in bowl for a while before serving to allow the dressing to permeate right through.

Main Courses

Savoury Bacon Flan

Prepare the flan case in advance and then you can finish off this dish in five minutes or so.

150 g (6 oz) wholemeal flour
½ teaspoon salt
75 g (3 oz) butter
1 egg

For the filling:
450 g (1 lb) cold boiled bacon
bunch spring onions
100 g (4 oz) button mushrooms
1 125-ml (¼-pint) carton yoghurt
seasoning
1 tablespoon chopped mint
few sprigs watercress

Sift the flour and salt into a bowl and rub in the butter until the mixture resembles fine breadcrumbs. Add the beaten egg and just sufficient water to mix to a stiff dough. Roll out to line a 17.5-cm (7-in) flan case. Prick the bottom of the pastry with a fork and cover with greaseproof paper and beans or lentils. Bake 'blind' at 190°C (375°F)/Gas 5 for 15 minutes, remove lentils and paper and allow to cool.

Chop the bacon into small dice. Top and tail the spring onions and chop them into small pieces. Slice the mushrooms. Combine the bacon, spring onions, mushrooms and yoghurt together. Stir in the chopped mint and season to taste. Just before serving, spoon the mixture into the flan case and decorate with sprigs of watercress around the edge and in the middle.

Pork Macaroni Pie

This is surprisingly filling, so serve it with a crisp green salad, or fresh green vegetables.

450 g (1 lb) cooked pork
2 tablespoons chopped fresh sage
2 medium-sized onions
50 g (2 oz) butter

80

25 g (1 oz) flour
250 ml (½ pint) milk
225 g (8 oz) quick-cooking macaroni
seasoning
50 g (2 oz) cheese

Preheat the oven to 200°C (400°F)/Gas 6. Cut the pork into small pieces. Chop the sage and sprinkle it over the pork. Melt half the butter in a pan and fry onions, finely chopped, until soft and golden. Cook the macaroni in the usual way, and drain.

Melt the remaining butter in a pan, remove from the heat and stir in the flour. Still stirring, add the milk. Return the pan to the heat and continue stirring until the sauce thickens.

In a deep, well-greased ovenproof casserole put a layer of macaroni, then a layer of pork, then all the onion. Season well between each layer. Add a further layer of macaroni, then one of pork, and finally top with remaining macaroni. Pour over the white sauce, top with grated cheese and cook in the oven for 25–30 minutes.

Pork'n'Beans

This sounds time-consuming, but if you start it in good time it's no trouble—and the flavour is delicious.

225 g (8 oz) haricot beans
1 rasher streaky bacon
1 teaspoon brown sugar
500 ml (1 pint) beef stock
675 g (1½ lb) belly pork
1 medium-sized onion
2 tablespoons tomato purée
225 g (8 oz) pork chipolatas

Soak the beans in cold water overnight. Next day, drain and put them in a saucepan with chopped bacon rasher, sugar and stock. Bring to a boil and simmer gently for 1½ hours.

In the meantime, cut the belly of pork into small 5-cm (2-in) pieces, removing any bone and gristle. Fry gently. Chop the onion and add it to pork, then add the tomato purée and cook for a few minutes. Into a deep casserole put a layer of meat, then beans, then meat, etc. ending with beans. Add a little more stock or water if necessary, to prevent sticking. Cook at 150°C (300°F)/Gas 2 for about 3 hours. An hour before serving, fry the sausages lightly, chop them into 2.5-cm (1-in) pieces and add them to the casserole.

Ginger-up Pork

50 g (2 oz) butter
2 cloves garlic
25 g (1 oz) fresh root ginger
4 spare-rib pork chops
½ teaspoon chilli powder
2 medium-sized onions
250 ml (½ pint) beef stock
1 tablespoon brown sugar
1 tablespoon Soy sauce
1 tablespoon flour

Melt the butter in a heavy saucepan and add the chopped garlic cloves. Then add the root ginger, grated or chopped very finely. Brown each chop on both sides, and when the juices have been sealed in, add chilli powder, sliced onions, stock, brown sugar, and Soy sauce. Cover and simmer gently for about 35 minutes or until chops are cooked. Remove them from the pan and keep hot. Blend a little of the liquid with the flour and stir into the sauce until it thickens. Replace the chops, and serve with boiled rice.

Honey Glaze Pork Chops

This has a spare-rib taste, but is made with full-sized pork chops to provide a hearty main meal.

4 pork chops
250 ml (½ pint) water
2 tablespoons cider vinegar
3 dessertspoons honey
1 dessertspoon Soy sauce
1 dessertspoon cornflour
seasoning
vegetable oil for frying

Put the pork chops in a saucepan with water and cider vinegar and bring to the boil. Simmer for 20 minutes, then drain chops and wipe them dry with kitchen paper. Mix honey, Soy sauce and cornflour together, and season. Coat the chops with the mixture on both sides.

Heat the oil in a frying pan and fry the chops on both sides until meat is tender. Serve with Savoury Rice (page 129).

Sausages'n'Cider

2 medium-sized onions
1 tablespoon vegetable oil

450 g (1 lb) pork sausages
1 large cooking apple
50 g (2 oz) mushrooms
250 ml (½ pint) dry cider such as Bulmer's Dry Reserve
seasoning

Peel and slice the onions. Heat the oil in a saucepan and fry onion until soft. Remove from pan. Fry sausages until brown on all sides. Peel, core and slice the cooking apple, and slice the mushrooms. Replace the onions in the pan, add the apple and mushrooms and pour in the cider. Season well. Bring to a boil and simmer very gently for 20 minutes. Stir from time to time with a wooden spoon to prevent sticking.

Noodle Mushroom Grill

You'll like this tasty way to serve noodles, especially if you cook the tagliatelli verdi (green noodles) which are on sale in many supermarkets now.

225 g (8 oz) noodles
50 g (2 oz) butter
1 large onion (finely chopped)
225 g (8 oz) mushrooms (sliced)
salt and pepper
50 g (2 oz) flour
1 teaspoon Worcestershire sauce
1 teaspoon Soy sauce
1 teaspoon dry mustard powder
500 ml (1 pint) milk
50 g (2 oz) grated Cheddar cheese

Cook the noodles as directed on the packet and keep them hot in a colander or sieve over a saucepan of hot water. Melt the butter in a saucepan, add the chopped onion. Cook slowly until soft. Add the sliced mushrooms. Cook for a few minutes more, then season well, and add the flour, sauces and mustard powder. Pour over the milk and stir well until mixture boils and thickens.

Remove the pan from the heat and stir in the noodles. Turn into a flameproof serving dish. Scatter the grated cheese on top and brown under the grill.

Lamb Cutlets in Curry Sauce

50 g (2 oz) dried apricots
2 medium-sized onions

25 g (1 oz) cooking fat
4 lamb cutlets
4 teaspoons curry powder
seasoning
250 ml ($\frac{1}{2}$ pint) stock
1 tablespoon chutney

Soak the apricots in cold water for 2–3 hours or overnight. Chop the onion finely. Heat the fat in a pan and fry the onion until soft but not brown. Add the cutlets and brown on both sides. Stir in the curry powder, seasoning and stock. Cover the pan tightly and simmer for 30 minutes. Drain the apricots, chop roughly, and add to the pan together with the chutney. Stir to mix, then cover the pan and cook for a further 15 minutes.

Lamb with Coriander

1 kg (2$\frac{1}{4}$ lb) scrag end of neck of lamb
2 medium-sized onions
2 tablespoons vegetable oil
2 cloves garlic
salt and pepper
$\frac{1}{4}$ teaspoon coriander seed
$\frac{1}{2}$ teaspoon turmeric
1 teaspoon Tabasco sauce
1 380-g (13$\frac{1}{2}$-oz) can tomatoes
250 ml ($\frac{1}{2}$ pint) stock

Chop the lamb into portion-sized pieces. Chop the onions finely. Heat the vegetable oil in a deep pan and fry the onions until soft but not brown. Add the chopped garlic, then the meat and fry until brown on both sides. Season with salt and pepper, add spices, Tabasco and stir. Finally add tomatoes and stock. Transfer to an ovenproof casserole and cook for 2$\frac{1}{4}$–2$\frac{1}{2}$ hours at 180° (350°F)/Gas 4.

Sweet'n'sour Lamb Cutlets

1 tablespoon oil
8 lamb cutlets (2 per person)
1 medium-sized onion
375 ml ($\frac{3}{4}$ pint) cold tea
2 tablespoons vinegar
1 tablespoon Soy sauce
1 tablespoon sugar
25 g (1 oz) grated root ginger
1 tablespoon cornflour

84

Heat the oil in a deep saucepan and fry the cutlets a few at a time until brown on both sides. Remove and put in an ovenproof casserole. Fry the chopped onion rings and add to the cutlets. Pour over the tea, vinegar, Soy sauce, sugar and grated root ginger. Mix thoroughly, then cover and cook at 180°C (350°F)/Gas 4 for 35–40 minutes. Blend the cornflour with a little of the liquid and return to casserole. Cover and cook for a further 15 minutes.

Chilli Con Carne

Here's a way of making the homely mince a little bit special. Red kidney beans are available now, either dried or canned, in many supermarkets.

75 g (3 oz) red kidney beans
2 medium-sized onions
2 tablespoons oil
450 g (1 lb) minced beef
1 tablespoon tomato purée
125 ml (¼ pint) beef stock
½ teaspoon chilli powder
salt

Soak the kidney beans in cold water overnight, or use canned kidney beans with the liquid drained. Chop the onions finely, and fry them in the oil until soft. Add beef and fry, stirring until just browned. Add tomato purée, stock, drained kidney beans, chilli powder and salt. Stir well. Bring to a boil, then turn down heat and cook very gently for about an hour or until the beans are cooked.

Beef Bacon and Apple Stew

4 rashers streaky bacon
450 g (1 lb) stewing steak
1 tablespoon chopped sage
salt and pepper
1 large onion
100 g (4 oz) mushrooms
500 ml (1 pint) beef stock
2 medium-sized cooking apples

Trim the bacon rinds, cut out the gristle, and cut the rashers into strips. Fry gently in a pan and when the fat is extracted, add the meat, cut into 5-cm (2-in) pieces. Add sage, seasoning, the onion peeled and sliced into rings, chopped mushrooms, beef stock, and stir well. Transfer to an ovenproof casserole. Cover and cook for 1½ hours at 180°C (350°F)/Gas 4.

Remove from oven. Wipe the apples and core and slice them, leaving the peel. Arrange the apple slices over the top of the casserole and spoon some of the stock over them. Replace the lid and continue cooking for a further 30 minutes.

Autumn Ragout

675 g (1½ lb) stewing beef
25 g cooking fat
12 baby onions
25 g (1 oz) flour
salt and pepper
500 ml (1 pint) beef stock
1 head celery
18 shelled chestnuts
rind and juice of 1 medium-sized orange

Brown the meat in the hot fat. Add the peeled onions and scatter the flour and seasoning over the pan. Pour in the stock, stir well, bring to the boil and allow to simmer for 1½–2 hours. Trim the celery head and cut it into four pieces. Add to the stew with the chestnuts and the grated rind and juice of the orange. Continue cooking for a further 30–40 minutes.

Chicken Cumin

1 1.35-kg (3-lb) chicken
rind and juice of ¼ lemon
25 g (1 oz) flour
½ teaspoon paprika
1 teaspoon cumin seeds
2 tablespoons oil
1 piece root ginger
250 ml (¼ pint) stock
salt and pepper
1 125-ml (5-oz) carton natural yoghurt

Cut the chicken into joints and sprinkle with lemon juice. Mix the flour with the paprika and cumin seeds. Coat each chicken joint with the seasoned flour. Heat the oil in a deep pan and fry the chicken joints until brown on both sides. Add the ginger, pour over the stock and add grated rind and any remaining juice from the lemon. Season with salt and pepper. Cover and cook over a low heat for about 50 minutes or until joints are cooked.

Remove the chicken and keep hot. Blend the carton of yoghurt with the liquid in the pan, reheat, but do not boil. Serve the chicken with the sauce over it, and accompanied by rice.

Chicken Seville

2 tablespoons vegetable oil
4 chicken portions
1 medium-sized onion
2 cloves garlic
1 red pepper (or use one from a can)
250 ml (½ pint) chicken stock
salt and pepper
20 green olives
1 tablespoon flour

Melt the oil in a pan and fry the chicken portions until they are brown on all sides. Remove and place in an ovenproof casserole. Fry the chopped onion and chopped garlic. Add sliced red pepper, chicken stock and seasoning. Cover the casserole and cook at 180°C (350°F)/Gas 4 for 45–50 minutes. Remove the casserole from the oven and add the olives. Blend 1 tablespoon flour with some of the liquid, beat until smooth, then stir into the casserole. Replace lid and return to the oven for a further 15 minutes.

Pigeon Pie

2 pigeons
1 carrot
1 medium-sized onion
1 bay leaf
seasoning
500 ml (1 pint) water
325 g (12 oz) pork sausage meat

For the shortcrust pastry:
100 g (4 oz) plain flour
½ teaspoon salt
25 g (1 oz) lard
25 g (1 oz) butter
egg yolk to glaze

Joint the pigeons and put all the joints and bones into a saucepan with the carrot and onions chopped into small pieces. Add bay leaf, seasoning and 500 ml (1 pint) water. Bring to a boil, reduce heat and simmer gently for about 30–40 minutes. Test to see that meat is cooked. Remove from the pan and take meat off the bone and chop it into small pieces. Add to sausage meat.

    Make the shortcrust pastry by mixing the flour and salt in a bowl, and gently rubbing in the fat. Add enough water to make a firm dough, and chill.

Pile the meat into a greased pie dish, season well, then add plenty of the stock. Roll out pastry to cover the pie dish. Put thin strips of pastry over edge of dish, sealing with water so that it adheres. Put the rest of the pastry over the top, seal firmly, and flute the edge. Using a sharp knife, make two or three slits in the centre. Brush the pastry with egg yolk to which a little salt and 1 teaspoon water have been added.

Bake at 220°C (425°F)/Gas 7, until pastry is golden brown—about 15 minutes.

Rabbit Breton-style

Rabbit often needs some extra flavouring especially if it isn't a wild one. It is well worth marinating the joints in advance.

For the marinade:
2 tablespoons oil
1 tablespoon vinegar
6 peppercorns
pinch salt
pinch mustard
pinch pepper
pinch sugar
2 bay leaves

1 rabbit cut into joints
100 g (4 oz) dried prunes
25 g (1 oz) flour
salt
pepper
tablespoon made English mustard
2 tablespoons oil
250 ml (½ pint) stock

Marinate the rabbit joints overnight. Soak the prunes in water or cold tea. The next day, remove the joints from the marinade, dry thoroughly and coat in seasoned flour. Spread each joint with made mustard. Brown the joints in the oil, add seasoning. Transfer to a casserole, add stock and cook at 160°C (325°F)/Gas 3 for 1½ hours. Add the prunes and cook for a further ½ hour.

Liver Risotto

For the rice:
2 tablespoons vegetable oil
125 g (5 oz) rice

1 280-g (10-oz) can tomatoes
2 teaspoons curry powder
500 ml (1 pint) beef stock
50 g (2 oz) mushrooms

For the fried liver:
2 tablespoons vegetable oil
25 g (1 oz) flour
seasoning
450 g (1 lb) lamb's liver

To make the risotto, heat the oil in a deep saucepan. Stir in the rice and fry gently for a few minutes, stirring with a wooden spoon to prevent sticking. Add tomatoes, curry powder and beef stock. Bring to a boil, then turn down the heat and simmer very gently until the rice has absorbed all the liquid—about 15 minutes. Stir from time to time to prevent sticking, and if necessary add a little water. Right at the end, add the coarsely chopped mushrooms and stir well in.

In the meantime, heat the remaining oil, roll the liver in seasoned flour and fry gently on both sides until cooked.

To serve, pile rice on a warmed serving dish and arrange liver in slices on top.

Tripe with Meat Balls

A German friend who came to stay taught me this way with tripe. It's an ideal recipe for serving tripe to anyone having it for the first time.

1 kg (2¼ lb) tripe
salt
1 large onion
sprig parsley
2 peppercorns
1 bay leaf
25 g (1 oz) butter
25 g (1 oz) flour
juice of ½ lemon
2 thick slices bread
450 g (1 lb) minced beef
1 egg
1 meat extract cube

Wash tripe well and plunge it into boiling salted water. Allow the water to come back to the boil, then remove tripe and rinse the pan. Into the rinsed pan put 500 ml (1 pint) cold water, salt, the onion, parsley, peppercorns, bay leaf, and the tripe. Bring to the boil, then reduce heat and simmer for about an hour or until tender. Strain the tripe, reserving the liquid, and cut it into thin strips.

Make a sauce by melting the butter in a pan. Remove from the heat, stir in the flour, and gradually add 375 ml ($\frac{3}{4}$ pint) liquid from the tripe. Return to heat and stir until sauce thickens. Season well, then add the lemon juice and tripe.

Make mincemeat balls by grating the bread and adding it to the minced beef. Season well, then mix with beaten egg. Form into small balls. Add to the tripe and cook for $\frac{1}{2}$ hour. Blend the meat extract cube with a little of the stock from the pan and stir in, blend well, then reheat and serve at once.

Autumn Mussels

Mussels make a surprisingly good and economical main meal, served simply on their own. If you like, you can serve them as a first course, using half quantities per person.

For each serving:
1 litre (1 quart) mussels
shallot or small onion
25 g (1 oz) butter
1 dessertspoon chopped parsley
1 wineglass dry white wine

Wash the mussels very thoroughly under running water. Discard any that are not tightly shut, and cut away the 'beard' or strands that appear to come from inside the shell. Scrub if necessary. Chop the onion and fry in a little butter until soft, add the chopped parsley and the wine.

Put the mussels into the pan, close the lid tightly and cook over a low heat for about 5 minutes. At the end of this time the shells should have opened. Lift the opened mussels in their shells on to a warm serving dish, and discard any that have not opened. Bring the liquor to the boil, pour it over the mussels, and serve at once.

These are usually eaten by picking them up in their shell and breaking the other part of the shell to use as a 'spoon'. Have a soup spoon handy as well to drink the remaining liquor which is delicious. Some people discard the empty half of the shells before serving but this is time consuming and not really necessary.

Brown bread and butter can be served as an accompaniment if you wish.

Onion and Anchovy Lattice Tart

Served with tomato salad and green peas this makes a delicious and economical meal.

For the cheese pastry:
225 g (8 oz) flour
1 teaspoon salt
100 g (4 oz) fat (preferably half lard, half butter)
75 g (3 oz) finely grated cheese
1 egg yolk
cold water to mix

For the filling:
450 g (1 lb) baby onions
50 g (2 oz) butter
1 tin anchovy fillets

To make the pastry, sieve the flour and salt into a bowl. Cut fat into small pieces and mix together until finely blended like breadcrumbs. Add the cheese. Mix with the egg yolk and enough water to make a stiff dough. Roll out to line a 20-cm (8-in) flan dish and prick the base. Fill base with greaseproof paper and lentils or beans, and bake 'blind' at 180°C (350°F)/Gas 4 for 20 minutes.

To make the filling, peel the onions and half cook them by boiling for 2–3 minutes. Drain thoroughly. Melt the butter, and when foaming add the onions to finish cooking over a gentle flame. Shake the pan regularly to ensure the onions cook evenly. Arrange onions in flan case and place the anchovy fillets in a lattice pattern over the top. Heat gently in a cool oven, 150°C (300°F)/Gas 2, until hot—about 20 minutes.

Haddock Cheese Flan

For the pastry:
150 g (6 oz) plain flour
½ teaspoon salt
75 g (3 oz) butter

For the filling:
325 g (12 oz) smoked haddock
250 ml (½ pint) milk
bay leaf
seasoning
1 tablespoon oil
1 medium-sized onion
2 standard eggs
50 g (2 oz) grated cheese

Preheat the oven to 190°C (375°F)/Gas 5. To make the pastry, sift the flour and salt into a bowl. Cut up the butter and mix with the flour, using your fingertips, until the mixture resembles fine breadcrumbs. Add enough cold water to make a firm dough. Roll out to line a 20-cm (8-in) flan ring. Prick the base with a fork, then cover with greaseproof paper and fill with dried beans or lentils to weight down the pastry. Bake 'blind' for 15 minutes. Remove greaseproof paper and lentils.

To make the filling, poach the fish in the milk with the bay leaf and seasoning. Drain, reserving the milk in which it has been cooked, and flake into pieces. Chop the onion and fry in the oil until it is soft but not coloured. Put onion in the bottom of the flan case and arrange the fish over the top. Beat the eggs together until yolk and white are mixed, then add the milk in which the fish was cooked. Pour carefully into the flan case, sprinkle the cheese on top. Heat in a warm oven, 160°C (325°F)/Gas 3 for 30 minutes.

Savoury Whiting in Choux Pastry

For the choux pastry:
125 ml (¼ pint) water
50 g (2 oz) butter
62.5 g (2½ oz) plain flour
2 standard eggs

For the savoury filling:
675 g (1½ lb) whiting
250 ml (½ pint) milk
2 tablespoons sage and onion stuffing
seasoning
25 g (1 oz) butter
25 g (1 oz) flour
50 g (2 oz) grated Cheddar cheese

Preheat the oven to 200°C (400°F)/Gas 6. Put water and butter in a pan and heat to boiling. Remove from the heat and pour in all the flour at once. Beat vigorously with a wooden spoon until the mixture is smooth and leaves the sides of the pan. Allow to cool a little. Beat the eggs together. When the mixture has cooled, add the beaten egg a little at a time, beating hard. The mixture should be glossy and stiff when egg has been absorbed.

Poach the whiting in the milk for about 15 minutes or until fish is just cooked. Drain, retaining the liquid. Flake the fish, and sprinkle with the sage and onion stuffing and seasoning. To make the cheese sauce, melt 25 g (1 oz) butter in a saucepan, remove from the heat and stir in flour. Gradually add 250 ml (½ pint) milk in which fish was cooked, stirring so that the mixture is smooth. Heat, stirring until sauce thickens. Add cheese, beat until smooth, then stir in fish.

Butter a 17-cm (7-in) pie dish and spread choux pastry around the edge, using the back of a spoon. Pile fish in the middle. Cover fish with buttered paper, leaving the pastry exposed, and cook at 200°C (400°F)/Gas 6 for 30 minutes.

Grey Mullet with Mushroom Stuffing

An unusual but beautifully flavoured fish to serve to guests. Once the scales have been removed the skin is most attractive. This recipe works equally well with bass.

1 grey mullet weighing about 900 g (2 lb)

For the court bouillon:
2 tablespoons cider vinegar
5 or 6 peppercorns
bay leaf
blade mace
salt

For the stuffing:
225 g (8 oz) mushrooms
little milk
2 tablespoons chopped fresh thyme
1 tablespoon cooked rice
2 tablespoons mayonnaise
4 or 5 olives (stoned and chopped)
2 or 3 sprigs parsley

De-scale the fish. The scales on grey mullet are extremely tough, and having scraped upwards from the tail using the back of a knife you will need to pick them off with your fingers.

Prepare the court bouillon by putting all the ingredients into a baking tin large enough to hold the fish. Add water to fill half the tin. Add the mullet and baste with the liquid. Preheat the oven to 190°C (375°F)/Gas 5. Cook the fish until the liquid begins to simmer (about 30 minutes). Drain fish and leave to become quite cold.

To make the stuffing, chop the mushrooms (leaving four or five aside) into three or four pieces, then poach in a little milk until just cooked. Drain thoroughly, then mix with chopped thyme, cooked rice and mayonnaise. Add the chopped olives.

To serve, put the fish on a serving dish, then gently press the stuffing into the cavity, and arrange the rest on the plate. Use the whole mushrooms as a garnish, and add sprigs of parsley.

Haddock and Bacon Gougère

Boiled bacon and haddock combine well with the cheese choux pastry to make a handsome looking main course.

For the cheese choux pastry:
125 ml (¼ pint) milk
50 g (2 oz) butter
62.5 g (2½ oz) plain flour
salt
2 standard eggs
50 g (2 oz) grated Cheddar cheese
¼ teaspoon mustard powder

For the filling:
225 g (8 oz) haddock
salt and pepper
1 thick slice boiled bacon (or use 3 cooked rashers back bacon)
2 tablespoons fruit chutney
25 g (1 oz) extra grated cheese for topping

Preheat oven to 200°C (400°F)/Gas 6. Place milk and butter in a saucepan. Bring to a boil, remove from heat, and add flour with a pinch of salt. Beat the mixture rapidly until it forms a solid dough. Leave to cool slightly. When cooled break the eggs into a bowl and blend together, then gradually add to the choux pastry beating well between each addition until the mixture is smooth and satiny. Add grated cheese and mustard powder.

Poach the haddock in a little water with salt and pepper. Drain and leave to cool. Remove any bones. Chop the bacon and mix with the fish. Add chutney and stir together. Season well.

Grease a 17.5-cm (7-in) flan tin and put the choux pastry mixture around the edge. Pour the fish and bacon mixture into the middle. Cover the centre with foil, leaving the choux pastry free. Bake for 35–40 minutes. Remove from oven.

Sprinkle grated cheese on top of the fish and brown under a hot grill before serving.

Desserts

Blackberry Mille Feuilles

Take this recipe in easy stages and it won't seem time consuming at all. Although flaky pastry is used here you can buy puff pastry to make it quicker and the result will be very similar.

For the flaky pastry:
225 g (8 oz) flour
½ teaspoon salt
75 g (2½ oz) butter
75 g (2½ oz) margarine
½ teaspoon lemon juice
125 ml (¼ pint) water

For the filling:
225 g (8 oz) blackberries
3 tablespoons water
25 g (1 oz) caster sugar
2 teaspoons arrowroot
125 ml (¼ pint) double cream

For the icing:
1 tablespoon water
1 teaspoon lemon juice
75–100 g (3–4 oz) icing sugar

To make the pastry, sieve the flour and salt into a bowl. Beat the butter and margarine together until well blended. Add lemon juice to the water, pour into the flour and mix into a dough. Knead gently until the dough is an even consistency.

Roll out the pastry to an oblong strip. Cut one-third of the fat into small pieces and put them over two-thirds of the dough. Fold the section of dough that is not covered with fat over the middle section, and fold the third dough section over that, to make an envelope shape. Seal the edges, turn once to the right. Press once or twice to help distribute the fat. Repeat the process twice more until all the fat has been used. It helps to chill the pastry between rollings. When finished, chill for at least twenty minutes.

Roll out very thinly, keeping the shape rectangular, and cut it into three even pieces. Place these on a baking tin and chill once more before baking.

Preheat the oven to 230°C (450°F)/Gas 8. Cook pastry for five minutes at that temperature, then lower heat to 190°C (375°F)/Gas 5 for a further 15 minutes. Cool on a wire rack.

Wash the blackberries and cook them in a pan with the water and sugar. Bring to a boil and simmer for a minute or two. Remove from heat. Take a little of the juice from the pan, to blend with the arrowroot. When this is smooth, pour it over the blackberries. Bring back to the boil, stirring until thickened. Pour into a bowl and allow to cool.

To assemble the cake, put one sheet of pastry on a cake plate and spared over half the blackberries. Whip the cream until stiff and spread half of it over the blackberries. Add the second pastry layer and repeat with the filling.

Cover the last pastry sheet with glacé icing by blending the water and lemon juice, then gradually beating in the icing sugar with a wooden spoon. Pour this over the top of the pastry and leave to set. Put the iced pastry sheet on top of the fruit layers. Serve by cutting with a very sharp knife.

Blackberry Kissel with Shortbread

You'll enjoy this combination of buttery shortbread with the sharpness of the blackberries.

For the shortbread:
100 g (4 oz) butter
50 g (2 oz) caster sugar
100 g (4 oz) plain flour
50 g (2 oz) semolina

For the blackberry kissel:
675 g (1½ lb) blackberries
125 ml (¼ pint) red wine or water (or use diluted Ribena)
25 g (1 oz) caster sugar
2 teaspoons arrowroot

Preheat the oven to 160°C (325°F)/Gas 3. Cream the butter and sugar until well blended. Gradually add the flour and semolina. Knead until it stays in one piece. Roll out to form a small round. Pinch the edges and prick the centre. Bake on a sheet covered with greaseproof paper, just below the centre of the oven, for 40–45 minutes. Remove the shortbread from the oven and mark into wedges whilst still warm. Do not cut it until just before serving.

To make the kissel, pick over the blackberries and wash them. Remove any tops and stalks. Put them into a saucepan with the red wine and nearly all the sugar, reserving a little to sprinkle over the cooked fruit. Bring to the boil, and allow to simmer for a minute or two. Strain the fruit into a bowl and retain the juice. Mix a little of the juice with the arrowroot and stir until well blended. Return to heat and add the rest of the juice. Stir vigorously until sauce has thickened, then pour over the berries. Sprinkle with remaining sugar to prevent a skin forming. Cool, then chill until ready to serve.

Chestnut Chantilly Meringue

2 egg whites
100 g (4 oz) caster sugar

For the filling:
225 g (8 oz) chestnuts
125 ml (¼ pint) double cream
2 teaspoons caster sugar
½ teaspoon vanilla essence

To make the meringue, whisk the egg whites until stiff. Add one-third of the sugar (judge the quantity by eye; there is no need to measure) and continue whisking until mixture peaks again. Add half the remaining sugar and whisk again. Add rest of the sugar by sprinkling it over the top of the mixture and whisking until the sugar is just absorbed.

Lightly oil two sheets of greaseproof paper and place each one on a baking sheet. Shape the meringue into eight pyramid-cones, using the backs of two spoons to do so. Place these on the baking sheets, leaving space between each meringue.

Cook at 120°C (250°F)/Gas ½ for two hours, then switch off the heat. Very carefully turn the meringues upside down and return them to the oven to allow them to dry out. The low temperature of your oven is essential if the meringues are to cook without becoming too brown. If necessary leave the oven door ajar while cooking to keep down the temperature.

To make the filling, wash the chestnuts and slit the skins. Boil for about ten minutes, then skin them and liquidise to a purée. You can if you wish use canned chestnut purée instead. Whip the cream until stiff, then add the sugar and vanilla essence and whisk for a few seconds more. Blend equal quantities of this chantilly cream with the chestnut purée. Sandwich together two meringue cones with this mixture, allowing about 1 cm (½ in) filling to each pair of meringues.

Harvest Sponge Pudding

For the topping:
375 g (¾ lb) plums
100 g (4 oz) blackberries
1 tablespoon honey
25 g (1 oz) butter

For the sponge:
225 g (8 oz) plain flour
½ teaspoon salt
2 teaspoons baking powder
75 g (3 oz) butter
75 g (3 oz) sugar
1 standard egg made up to 125 ml (¼ pint) with milk

Halve and stone the plums and stew them in a very little water until cooked. Sweeten if necessary. Wash the blackberries. Put the honey and butter in a small pan and heat until blended, then pour into the bottom of a 1-litre (2-pint) greased pudding basin. Add half the plums and half the blackberries.

To make the sponge mixture, sieve flour, salt and baking powder together. Rub in the butter. Add the sugar. Blend the egg with the milk and mix with the flour to make a soft dough. Pile over the fruit. Cover and steam in a pan half full of boiling water for 1¼ hours.

To serve, turn the pudding out on to a plate. Heat the remaining plums and blackberries and serve these separately.

Brandy Plum Sandwich

Make the sponge cake on the same day you intend to serve this dessert; since it is without fat, the cake soon dries.

For the brandied plums:
450 g (1 lb) dark plums
175 g (7 oz) granulated sugar
125 ml (¼ pint) water
1 tablespoon brandy

For the sponge cake:
3 standard eggs
75 g (3 oz) caster sugar
¼ teaspoon vanilla essence
75 g (3 oz) flour (or you can use equal weights of egg, sugar and flour if it is easier)

Halve and stone the plums. Put the sugar and water in a saucepan and heat gently until sugar has dissolved. Add the plums and poach gently in the syrup for about 5 minutes or until the plums are soft. Add the brandy. Cool, then chill, preferably overnight.

The next day, grease and line a 17.5-cm (7-in) cake tin. Preheat oven to 190°C (375°F)/Gas 5. Break the eggs into a bowl and whisk lightly until blended. Add sugar and vanilla essence and whisk over hot water until the mixture is thick and creamy and will leave a trail. If you have an electric mixer the hot water is unnecessary. Fold in the flour, using a metal spoon. Use a light touch and stir only sufficiently to blend.

Turn into the prepared cake tin and turn the oven down to 180°C (350°F)/Gas 4. Cook for 20 minutes or until the cake slightly shrinks from the sides of the tin. Allow to cool in the tin for a few minutes before inverting on to a wire rack to cool completely.

To assemble, cut the cake in two right through the middle to make two rounds. Put one round on to a plate. Drain the plums, reserving the juice, and spoon half the plum juice over the cake to moisten. Use half the plums as a filling, saving the best shaped plums for the top layer. Top with the second cake and repeat with the remaining juice and top with the plums. Serve with cream or ice-cream.

Plum Pudding

Not the type we usually mean but a delicious, quickly assembled pudding that the family will find very tasty.

300 g (10 oz) stale cake (use Madeira for preference)
4 tablespoons sweet white wine
2 tablespoons clear honey
450 g (1 lb) plums stewed with sugar to taste
125 ml (¼ pint) double cream

Crumble the cake into crumbs. Heat the wine and honey together just sufficiently to blend. Stew the plums in a little water and stone them.

Into a 1-litre (2-pint) pudding basin put half the crumbs. Moisten with half the wine and honey, then spoon over half the plums. Add the remaining crumbs, moisten with the rest of the wine and spoon over the plums. Weight down with a saucer topped with a ½-kg (1-lb) weight and leave in a refrigerator overnight. This will ensure that the cake crumbs do not separate from the juice, and that the pudding will hold its shape.

To serve, carefully invert the pudding on to a plate. Whip the cream and either use it to coat the pudding or serve it separately.

Apple Macaroon Layer

If you make the apple purée in advance, this sweet can literally be assembled in minutes.

450 g (1 lb) cooking apples
4 large macaroons
125 ml (¼ pint) natural yoghurt
2 teaspoons brown sugar

Peel and core the apples. Put them in a saucepan with a tablespoon of water, cover and cook gently until soft. Beat with a wooden spoon to make a smooth purée. Cool, then chill.

Crumble the macaroons into small pieces, stir in to the yoghurt, and add the brown sugar. Layer the apple and yoghurt mixture into four wine glasses, starting with an apple layer, then yoghurt, and continuing to the top.

Chocolate Cream

A very rich dessert, ideal after a fairly light main course.

3 large eggs
75 g (3 oz) sugar
50 g (2 oz) plain chocolate
2 tablespoons water
125 ml (¼ pint) double cream

Separate the eggs. Whisk the egg yolks and sugar together until white and creamy. In a basin, melt the chocolate in 2 tablespoons water. Heat over hot water and stir until blended. Cool slightly, then add to the egg yolks. Whisk the cream until stiff and beat it into the chocolate mixture. Whisk the egg whites until they form peaks, then lightly fold into chocolate, using a metal spoon.

Pour into a bowl, smooth the top and chill in the refrigerator for at least three hours.

Ginger Grape Cream

100 g (4 oz) ginger biscuits
225 g (8 oz) black grapes
1 125-ml (¼-pint) carton sour cream
1 125-ml (¼-pint) carton natural yoghurt
2 tablespoons demerara sugar

Put the ginger biscuits into a bag and crush them with a rolling pin. Cut the grapes in half lengthwise and de-pip them, but leave the skins on. Combine the sour cream and yoghurt and stir together until blended. Into 4 glasses (or cocotte dishes) spoon a layer of crumbs followed by grapes followed by the sour cream and yoghurt mixture. Layer up until the glasses are full, finishing with a cream layer. Chill thoroughly and just before serving sprinkle the demerara sugar on top.

Almond Cream

Simple and very quick to prepare, this is a deliciously creamy dessert.

2 large eggs and 1 yolk
25 g (1 oz) sugar
½ teaspoon almond essence
375 ml (¾ pint) milk
2 tablespoons apricot or raspberry jam

Whisk together the eggs, sugar and almond essence until well blended. Warm the milk to blood heat, pour over the eggs and stir.

Butter a 15-cm (6-in) ovenproof dish. Spread the bottom with jam, then pour over the milk and egg mixture. Cover with foil or greaseproof paper. Stand in a baking dish half full of water and cook at 180°C (350°F)/Gas 4 for 45–50 minutes.

Greengage Cream

Greengages are still around in early autumn, so do make this lovely dessert when you can.

450 g (1 lb) greengages
125 ml (¼ pint) water
2 tablespoons sugar
250 ml (½ pint) thick custard
4 tablespoons water
12.5 g (½ oz) gelatine
125 ml (¼ pint) double cream
few drops green food colouring

Put the greengages in a saucepan with the 125 ml (¼ pint) water and sugar. Simmer gently until soft. Press through a nylon sieve and allow the purée to cool. Make the custard in the usual way and cover with wet greaseproof paper to prevent a skin forming. Put the 4 tablespoons water in a mug, sprinkle the gelatine over and dissolve by standing the mug in a pan of water and heating gently. Mix the custard with the fruit purée, and when the gelatine has cooled a little stir it into the mixture. Whip the cream until stiff and fold in. Add a few drops of green colouring and stir until thoroughly blended.

Wet a 750-ml (1½-pint) jelly mould and pour in the mixture. Allow to set, then turn out and serve with cream.

Syllabub

This is the one time in this book that I've broken the rule not to use more than 125 ml (¼ pint) double cream, but there's no point making a syllabub without double this quantity. As it's so rich, serve it in small glasses.

1 medium-sized lemon
125 ml (¼ pint) cider such as Bulmer's Woodpecker
50 g (2 oz) caster sugar
1 tablespoon brandy or ½ teaspoon brandy essence
250 ml (½ pint) double cream

Finely grate the lemon rind, then cut the lemon in half and squeeze out the juice. Put in a bowl with the rind, cider, sugar and brandy or brandy essence. Cover and leave for a few hours.

Combine the cream and the cider liquid in a large bowl and whisk steadily, using a balloon whisk if you have one, until the mixture forms soft peaks. Spoon carefully into glasses and serve.

You can make this a few hours beforehand and chill if you wish. Serve with lemon sponge fingers.

Banana Cream Whip

This rich dessert is very quick to prepare.

4 ripe bananas
juice of ½ lemon
2 tablespoons redcurrant or crab apple jelly
white of 1 standard egg
125 ml (¼ pint) double cream

Peel and mash the bananas and sprinkle them with the lemon juice. Beat in the redcurrant jelly. Add the egg white to the double cream and whip until stiff. Fold all but two dessertspoons into the banana mixture. Spoon into wine glasses and chill until ready to serve. Just before taking the desserts to the table, spoon a swirl of cream over each one.

Hazelnut Soufflé

50 g (2 oz) hazelnuts
12.5 g (½ oz) gelatine
3 large eggs
75 g (3 oz) caster sugar
125 ml (¼ pint) double cream

Prepare a 15-cm (6-in) soufflé dish by tightly tying a band of greaseproof paper around it so that it stands about 5 cm (2 in) above the dish.

Toast the hazelnuts under a grill, or leave for 5–10 minutes in the top of a warm oven. Rub between a cloth so that the outer skin is removed, then chop very finely. This is easiest if you use a wet knife.

Dissolve gelatine in 2 tablespoons water. To do this, put the water in a cup, sprinkle the gelatine over the water and heat gently by standing the cup in hot water until the gelatine granules are dissolved.

Separate the eggs. Whisk the egg yolks and sugar over hot water until white and creamy and the mixture leaves a trail. Remove from heat, then continue to whisk until cold. (If you have an electric whisk you do not need to put the bowl over hot water.) Add two-thirds of the chopped nuts.

Whip the cream until stiff and whisk the egg whites until they are stiff enough to form peaks.

Pour the gelatine in a thin stream into the egg yolks and stir gently with a metal spoon. Fold in three quarters of the cream and all the egg whites. Mix in very lightly, just sufficiently to blend the ingredients.

Pour into the soufflé dish and leave to set.

Just before serving, remove the paper very carefully by peeling it back with the aid of a knife. Decorate with remaining cream and make a pattern with the rest of the chopped nuts.

Pear and Prune Compote

The contrast of the juicy pears and the dark prunes looks very attractive when served in a shallow dish.

225 g (8 oz) prunes
250 ml (½ pint) cold tea
4 large ripe pears
½ lemon

Soak the prunes overnight in cold tea. Next day, peel and core the pears and rub them with lemon to prevent discolouring. If the pears prove to be unripe when cut, poach them in a little sugar and water until they are soft. Cook the prunes in a little of the cold tea, adding the lemon rind cut into strips. Chill both the pears and the prunes very thoroughly in separate dishes until ready to serve.

Put the pears in the middle of a shallow dish and arrange the prunes around the edge. Serve with plenty of cream.

Spiced Pears

Windfall pears, slightly under-ripe, are just right for this dish and make it quite economical even though you use red wine.

675 g (1½ lb) pears
250 ml (½ pint) red wine
1 2.5-cm (1-in) cinnamon stick (or ½ teaspoon powdered cinnamon)
4 or 5 cloves
1 tablespoon marmalade
sugar to taste

Peel, core and slice the pears and put them immediately into salted water to prevent discolouring. Put the wine, spices and marmalade into a saucepan, add the drained pears and sugar if required. Poach gently until pears are cooked. Put them into a bowl, pour the strained wine over and chill thoroughly until ready to serve.

Apple Water Ice

Even on cool autumn nights, ices can be a welcome dessert.

450 g (1 lb) cooking apples
50 g (2 oz) sugar
juice of 1 lemon
12.5 g (½ oz) gelatine
1 tablespoon finely chopped mint
green colouring
1 standard egg white

Turn the freezer compartment of your refrigerator to its coldest setting. Chop the apples but do not peel or core them. Cook in a very little water until soft, then put through a sieve. Add sugar. Squeeze the lemon juice into a cup and add water to make up to 3 tablespoons. Sprinkle gelatine into this, and stand the cup in a pan of hot water over a gentle heat until the gelatine has dissolved. Stir into the apple purée with the chopped mint and a few drops of green food colouring. Pour into freezing trays and put in the freezer compartment until mushy—about 2–3 hours.

Whisk the egg white until stiff, stir in to the frozen apple and refreeze.

Plum Condé

Rice tinged with pink and the strong red of plums makes this a colourful dish to serve during early autumn.

225 g (8 oz) plums
50 g (2 oz) granulated sugar
125 ml (¼ pint) water

For the rice condé:
50 g (2 oz) round grain rice
50 g (2 oz) sugar
few drops vanilla essence
500 ml (1 pint) milk
12.5 g (½ oz) gelatine
1 tablespoon cream

Cut plums into halves and stone them. Dissolve the sugar in water over a low heat and bring to the boil. Add the plums and poach them gently until they are cooked but still hold their shape. Drain the juice and reserve it in a cup. Leave plums to cool.

Put rice, sugar, vanilla essence and some of the milk into a pan. Bring to the boil and add more milk. Stir to prevent sticking. Simmer very gently on top of the stove for about $\frac{1}{2}$–$\frac{3}{4}$ hour (use a heat mat if you have one). During this time gradually add the remaining milk until the rice has absorbed it all and is thick and creamy. Leave to cool.

Sprinkle the gelatine into the juice from the plums and dissolve it by standing the cup in a pan of hot water and heating gently. When dissolved, stir into the rice and add the tablespoon of cream.

Cover the bottom of a 17.5-cm (7-in) ring mould with the plums, overlapping and cut side up. Pour in the rice, smooth down with a spoon and leave to set.

Turn out and serve with cream.

Orange Flan

This flan can be served hot or cold depending on the weather.

150 g (6 oz) plain flour
$\frac{1}{4}$ teaspoon salt
75 g (3 oz) butter

For the filling:
3 oranges
250 ml ($\frac{1}{2}$ pint) diluted orange squash
50 g (2 oz) semolina
25 g (1 oz) butter
2 standard eggs
100 g (4 oz) caster sugar

To make the pastry case, sift the flour and salt into a bowl and rub in the butter with your fingertips until the mixture resembles fine breadcrumbs. Add enough water to mix to a stiff dough. Roll out to line a 17.5-cm (7-in) flan dish and bake 'blind' at 190°C (375°F)/Gas 5 for about 15 minutes. Remove and allow to cool.

Peel and coarsely chop the oranges. Put the orange squash into a saucepan, scatter over the semolina and stir over a gentle heat until the liquid thickens. Leave to cool, then beat in the softened butter. Separate egg whites from yolks. Beat in egg yolks and 50 g (2 oz) sugar. Add the chopped orange segments.

Turn down the oven to 150°C (300°F)/Gas 2.

Whisk the egg whites until they form peaks. Fold in one-third of the remaining sugar and beat again until mixture is satiny. Then add half the remaining sugar, beat again, and sprinkle over the rest of the sugar.

Pour the orange mixture into the pie case, pile meringue on top and set meringue in the fairly cool oven for about 20 minutes.

Plum Cheesecake

The plums should be fairly sweet to contrast well with the cheesecake. Add more sugar if you know you have a sweet tooth.

1 packet orange jelly
250 ml (½ pint) water
225 g (8 oz) curd cheese
225 g (8 oz) cream cheese
1 125-ml (¼-pint) carton natural yoghurt
450 g (1 lb) cooking plums
50 g (2 oz) granulated sugar

Dissolve jelly in the 250 ml (½ pint) water. Blend curd and cream cheese together, add yoghurt and stir into the jelly. If necessary sieve to make a smooth blend. Turn into a dish and leave to set.

Halve and stone the plums. Poach in a little water with the sugar until they are cooked but still hold their shape. Turn out into a dish and cool, then chill.

Put some of the plums over the top of the cheesecake and serve the rest as an accompaniment.

Winter in our house is definitely not a time for lurking overlong around the kitchen. Since we've had a cat-flap the draught blows around one's ankles and it's a case of long skirts and fleecy slippers or standing on an orange box to avoid it. In any case, working wives know the energy-saving value of nourishing casseroles that can be cooked while the oven is on for something else and reheated the next day before serving.

Root vegetables, sprats and hare are all good value during these months. Make the most of the vegetables available to serve simple starters, not forgetting the host of soups that can be made with winter roots. This is a time to be economical, to cut down on the quantities of meat you use to feed the family and use more vegetables to fill them up instead. Cheap cuts casserole beautifully, and don't be afraid to ask the butcher for help if you're unsure. Chicken remains a good inexpensive base for many meals, although in these days of battery hens one needs to spice it up a bit—try Chicken the French Way or Chicken Rama to see how versatile poultry can be.

Don't forget all the lovely citrus fruits that appear so colourfully in the shops at this time. Use them for marmalades (see Jams, Chutneys and Jelly chapter), or make use of them in a variety of desserts from Orange Foam to a warming Marmalade Sponge.

Starters

Carrot and Orange Soup

An unusual flavour that will intrigue your guests.

1 medium-sized onion
450 g (1 lb) carrots
25 g (1 oz) butter
salt and pepper
500 ml (1 pint) chicken stock
rind and juice of 1 medium-sized orange
125 ml (¼ pint) milk

Chop the onion and peel and thinly slice the carrots. Melt the butter in a saucepan and gently soften the onion, but do not allow it to brown. Add the carrots and season with salt and pepper. Pour in the stock, bring to a boil, cover and cook for 20 minutes or until the carrots are tender. Grate the rind of the orange and add to the soup, then extract the juice and add that as well, stirring until the ingredients are well blended.

Sieve or liquidise in a blender if you have one. Return the soup to the pan, add milk and reheat slowly, adjusting seasoning if necessary.

Artichoke Soup

This is one of the nicest soups I know. Thick, warm and comforting on a cold day, it has a really unique flavour.

3 medium-sized onions
450 g (1 lb) Jerusalem artichokes
25 g (1 oz) butter
500 ml (1 pint) chicken stock
salt
pepper
2 bay leaves
125 ml (¼ pint) milk

Chop the onions. Scrub the artichokes and cut them into small pieces. Melt the butter in a saucepan, add onions and fry until soft but not golden. Add the artichokes and fry gently for a few more minutes. Pour in the stock, season well, add bay leaves and bring to the boil. Reduce heat and simmer gently for about 20 minutes. Press through a sieve or use a blender if you have one. Reheat, adding the milk. Adjust seasoning as necessary.

Chestnut Soup

Its distinctive nutty flavour makes this soup really delicious. It needs no thickening. Although the preparation is time consuming, it really is worth while.

450 g (1 lb) chestnuts
25 g (1 oz) butter
salt and pepper
1 litre (2 pints) chicken stock
125 ml (¼ pint) milk

Rinse the chestnuts in cold water to clean the shells. Slit the shells, then put the nuts into boiling water and simmer for about 10 minutes to soften them. Skin and chop nuts, discarding any brown pieces.

Melt the butter in a pan, and fry the chestnuts very gently for about 5 minutes. Add seasoning and the stock. Bring to a boil, stirring, then cover and simmer for about 20 minutes.

Blend to a purée in a liquidiser, or rub through a sieve by pressing with the back of a wooden spoon. Reheat, adding milk, and serve.

Thick Vegetable Soup

This is the sort of soup to have when you've come home thoroughly chilled from a walk or a football match. The quantities given make it very thick, but you can add extra milk or water as required when reheating.

50 g (2 oz) lentils
450 g (1 lb) mixed root vegetables such as carrot, swede and turnip
2 medium-sized onions
25 g (1 oz) butter
750 ml (1½ pints) water
salt and pepper

Soak the lentils overnight, then drain. Next day, peel the root vegetables and chop them into medium-sized pieces. Peel and chop the onion finely. Melt the butter in a pan, and fry the onions until softened. Add the vegetables, then the lentils. Season and pour in the water. Bring to a boil and simmer for 20 minutes. Blend or press through a sieve. Adjust seasoning, reheat and serve.

Terrine of Hare

Personally I think it's extravagant to use a whole hare for making a pâté, but this recipe takes a small amount from a good carcass and leaves the main part for a delicious casserole (see page 124).

300 g (11 oz) hare meat
125 ml (¼ pint) red wine
1 tablespoon chopped parsley and thyme
black pepper
salt
225 g (8 oz) pork sausage meat
5 rashers streaky bacon

Cut the flesh from bones and chop into small 1.5-cm (½-in) pieces. Marinate in the red wine for about 2 hours with black pepper, salt and chopped herbs sprinkled over.

Mix the flesh with sausage meat, add extra seasoning. Line a ½-kg (1-lb) loaf tin with foil, then put streaky bacon at the bottom and around the sides. Spread the meat mixture over the bacon and press well down. Cover carefully with more foil to seal thoroughly.

Half fill a baking tin with cold water, then place the loaf tin in the centre and cook in the middle of moderate oven, 180°C (350°F)/Gas 5, for 1 hour. Remove from oven and leave in the tin until the terrine is cold.

Sprats

Serve these small fish whole. Most people will remove the heads and eat the rest, bones and all.

450 g (1 lb) sprats
flour
salt and pepper

To garnish:
1 lemon
brown bread and butter

Wash the sprats and dry them in kitchen paper or a clean cloth. Coat them in the seasoned flour. Rub a heavy-based frying pan with salt, then discard the salt. Add fresh salt to lightly coat the bottom of the pan. Add the sprats to the pan a few at a time and gently dry fry them until cooked on one side. Turn them carefully so as not to pierce the skin. As they are cooked remove and keep hot. Repeat with remaining fish.

Serve with wedges of thinly cut brown bread and butter and wedges of lemon.

Sprats in Soy Sauce

Dressed in this way, the homely sprat takes on an oriental flavour.

450 g (1 lb) sprats
1 tablespoon Soy sauce
juice of 1 lemon
2 cloves garlic
½ teaspoon ground ginger

Thoroughly wash the sprats and dry on kitchen paper or a clean cloth. Put them in a shallow ovenproof dish. Mix Soy sauce, lemon juice, chopped garlic and ginger together and pour over the fish. Cover and leave to marinate for 2–3 hours. Cook, covered, for 20 minutes at 180°C (350°F)/Gas 4. Serve with wedges of lemon and thinly sliced toast.

Leeks in Cheese Sauce

8 leeks
25 g (1 oz) butter
25 g (1 oz) flour

250 ml (½ pint) milk
125 g (5 oz) Cheddar cheese (grated)

Trim and top and tail the leeks to remove any blemished outer skin. Wash them well and leave in one piece. Put the leeks into boiling salted water and simmer for 10–15 minutes, depending on their size, until just tender. Drain and keep hot.

To make the cheese sauce, melt the butter in a saucepan, remove from heat and blend in the flour. Gradually add the milk, stirring all the time to make a smooth mixture. Return the pan to the heat and stir continually until the sauce has thickened. Add two-thirds of the grated cheese and beat the sauce until cheese has blended.

Arrange the leeks in a flameproof dish. Spoon the sauce over and sprinkle the remaining cheese on top. Brown under the grill and serve at once.

Parsnips in Sour Cream

The sweet-sour taste of this starter is unusual—and it's no trouble at all to make.

4 medium-to-large parsnips
1 125-ml (¼-pint) carton sour cream
grated nutmeg

Scrape the parsnips and trim and cut each one lengthways into four slices. Put them in cold water, bring to a boil and simmer for 10 minutes or until cooked.

In a separate pan, heat the sour cream until quite hot and of a liquid consistency, but do *not* allow to boil. Drain the parsnips and add to cream. Serve sprinkled generously with nutmeg.

Cauliflower Surprise

The secret of this recipe is to get everything ready at the same time to save reheating it in the oven.

150 g (6 oz) long grain rice
1 cauliflower
100 g (4 oz) ham
25 g (1 oz) butter
25 g (1 oz) flour
250 ml (½ pint) milk
50 g (2 oz) Cheddar cheese (grated)
2 firm tomatoes

Pour the rice into a pan of boiling salted water. Cook for 12 minutes, stirring with a fork from time to time to prevent sticking. Into another pan of boiling water, put the cauliflower cut into small florets. Simmer until just cooked. Chop the ham. Melt the butter in a pan, remove from the heat and stir in the flour. Gradually add the milk, stirring to avoid lumps. Return the pan to the heat and bring to the boil, stirring all the time until sauce thickens. Add three-quarters of the grated cheese and stir in well.

When the rice has cooked, drain into a sieve and run hot water through it to separate the grains. Put the rice at the bottom of a serving dish. Drain the cooked cauliflower and place on top of the rice. Scatter over the chopped ham, then pour over the cheese sauce. Place the remaining cheese on top and brown under the grill. Garnish the dish with thin slices of tomato.

Mushrooms in Garlic Butter

225 g (8 oz) mushrooms
2 cloves garlic
50 g (2 oz) butter
salt and pepper
2 tablespoons chopped parsley

Slice the mushrooms. Finely chop the garlic, or use a garlic press if you have one. Melt the butter in a pan and add the garlic, then gently fry the mushrooms until they are coated with butter and just cooked through. Season with salt and pepper. Serve at once, sprinkled with chopped parsley. Fresh French bread makes a good accompaniment.

Peking Pork

These quantities can be doubled to make a delicious main meal.

2 large pork chops
1 tablespoon cooking oil
2 cloves garlic
25 g (1 oz) peanuts
1 tablespoon Soy sauce
1 tablespoon sugar
2 oranges
100 g (4 oz) long grain rice

Cut the meat from the chops into 1.25-cm ($\frac{1}{2}$-in) pieces. Heat the oil in a pan, add the chopped garlic and pork and cook, stirring from time to time, for about 10 minutes. Add the peanuts, Soy sauce and sugar and blend together. Peel the oranges removing the pith, and cut into segments.

Boil the rice in salted water for 12 minutes. Test to see if it is cooked by crushing a grain between your fingers. Drain the rice and run hot water through it to remove starchy liquid.

Serve the pork on a bed of rice and arrange the orange segments as a decoration on top.

Cheese and Thyme Soufflé

Hot soufflés won't wait for anyone, so make sure the recipients are already sitting at the table.

225 g (8 oz) cream cheese
1 125-ml (5-oz) carton sour cream
3 eggs
seasoning
1 tablespoon chopped thyme

Prepare a 15-cm (6-in) soufflé dish by tightly tying a band of greaseproof paper around it, so that the paper stands at least 2 inches above the dish. Heat the oven to 180°C (350°F)/Gas 4.

Beat the cheese well with a wooden spoon until it is soft and smooth. Add the sour cream a little at a time, beating well. Separate the eggs. Add the yolks to the cheese, one at a time, thoroughly beating each one into the mixture. Whisk egg whites until stiff, so that they form peaks. Fold them into the cheese mixture, using a metal spoon. Add chopped thyme and seasoning, then pour into the prepared soufflé dish.

Cook for 30–35 minutes and serve at one.

Apple and Cucumber Salad

2 large dessert apples
⅓ medium-sized cucumber
1 125-ml (¼-pint) carton sour cream
4 slices black bread (Danish rye bread works well)
butter for spreading
1 tablespoon chopped parsley

Wipe the apples to clean their skins. Core and slice thinly, leaving the peel intact. Drop immediately into salted water to prevent them browning. Slice the cucumber very thinly, use a slicing gadget if you have one. Drain the apple slices, mix with the cucumber in a bowl and then pour in the sour cream. Lightly butter four slices of black bread, and just before serving arrange the apple and cucumber on the bread. Sprinkle with chopped parsley.

Main Courses

Pork Chops with Almond Butter

An unusual combination of ingredients to upgrade a plain pork chop.

1 tablespoon mustard powder
1 tablespoon brown sugar
1 teaspoon powdered ginger
seasoning
4 pork chops
50 g (2 oz) butter
50 g (2 oz) chopped almonds

Mix the mustard powder with the brown sugar, ginger and seasoning. Rub the mixture into both sides of chops. Dot with a little of the butter and cook under the grill, turning as necessary.

In the meantime, melt the remaining butter in a pan and fry the almonds. When the chops are cooked pour over the buttered almonds and serve.

Pork Chops En Croutte

The addition of pastry makes this a very substantial meal.

4 small pork chops
350 g (12 oz) puff pastry
4 dessertspoons Branston pickle
milk or beaten egg for glaze

Preheat oven to 220°C (425°F)/Gas 7. Trim the pork chops of most of the fat. Roll out the pastry thinly, so that it can be divided into four portions. Place one chop on the centre of each, top with a dessertspoon of pickle, then fold the pastry over, sealing all the edges firmly, so that each chop is completely enclosed. Put them on a baking tray, and brush the pastry with a little milk or beaten egg.

Cook for 20 minutes in the preheated oven, then reduce heat to 190°C (375°F)/Gas 5 for a further 20 minutes.

Sweet Pork Casserole

Spicy pork that gives the chops a fancy taste.

4 pork chops
1 tablespoon cooking oil

2 cooking apples
50 g (2 oz) sultanas
1 level teaspoon chopped sage
3 tablespoons honey
2 tablespoons cider vinegar
4 tablespoons water
seasoning

Trim fat from pork. Heat the oil in a pan and briefly fry the pork to seal in the juices. Transfer to an ovenproof casserole. Peel the apples, core and slice them thinly, and arrange over the pork. Add the sultanas, sage, honey, cider vinegar and water. Season well. Cover with a tight fitting lid, then cook for 1 hour at 180°C (350°F)/Gas 4. Check during cooking to see that too much moisture hasn't evaporated, and if necessary add a little more water.

Cassoulet

A hearty peasanty casserole that's surprisingly tasty and not too expensive.

225 g (8 oz) butter beans
225 g (8 oz) onions
900 g (2 lb) belly of pork
1 tablespoon cooking oil
225 g (8 oz) garlic sausage in one piece
1 225-g (8-oz) can tomatoes
500 ml (1 pint) stock
salt and pepper
3 thick slices bread made into breadcrumbs

Soak the butter beans in cold water overnight. Next day, chop the onions finely. Cut up the belly of pork into 2.5-cm (1-in) pieces, discarding any bone. Heat the oil in a deep casserole or pan and fry the chopped onion until soft. Add the pork and cook, turning meat so that it is brown all over. (It is always best to stir with a wooden spoon so that the juices are retained in the meat.) Add the drained butter beans.

Chop the garlic sausage into small cubes—about 1.25-cm ($\frac{1}{2}$-in)—and add to the pan, together with the tomatoes, stock, and seasoning. Bring to a boil, stirring well, then transfer the mixture to an ovenproof casserole and cover.

Cook at 160°C (325°F)/Gas 3 for 2 hours. Sprinkle the top with the breadcrumbs and then continue cooking, uncovered, for a further half hour to crisp up the breadcrumbs. These soak up any excess fat and give the cassoulet a lovely golden crust.

Sausage and Cabbage Casserole

Very easy to make, this dish is just right for eating round the fire on a cold evening.

450 g (1 lb) pork chipolatas
2 medium-sized onions
325 g (¾ lb) shredded white cabbage
375 ml (¾ pint) chicken stock
1 teaspoon chopped herbs such as parsley and thyme
4 slices French bread spread with butter and English mustard

Grill the sausages until brown on the outside. Chop the onions. Put a layer of shredded cabbage at the bottom of an ovenproof dish. Add a layer of onions and then a layer of sausages (cut into 2.5-cm (1-in) slices). Continue in layers, ending with cabbage. Be sure to season each layer well with salt and pepper. Sprinkle chopped herbs over the top and pour in the stock. Cover and cook at 180°C (350°F)/Gas 4 for 45 minutes. Remove lid from casserole and add French bread, buttered side up, pressing the slices down with a spoon so that the bread absorbs some of the liquid. Return to oven uncovered and cook for a further 15 minutes.

Beef with Prunes and Frankfurters

The prunes and frankfurters blend to make this a very special dish.

100 g (4 oz) dried prunes
675 g (1½ lb) stewing beef
2 medium-sized onions
2 tablespoons oil
250 ml (½ pint) red wine or beef stock
seasoning
1 small can or packet frankfurters

Soak the prunes overnight in water or cold tea. Cut up the meat into 8 portions. Chop the onions finely and fry them gently in oil, then add the meat and brown it on all sides. (Use a wooden spoon for stirring so that the juices in the meat are sealed.) Transfer to an ovenproof dish, add wine or stock and season well. Cover and put into a moderate oven, 180°C (350°F)/Gas 4, for 2 hours. Remove from oven, add prunes and frankfurters chopped into 2.5-cm (1-in) pieces. Continue cooking for further ½ hour.

Carbonnade of Beef

The lovely dark sauce from the brown ale makes the meat look and taste rich.

675 g (1½ lb) stewing steak
2 medium-sized onions
25 g (1 oz) flour
seasoning
25 g (1 oz) cooking fat
250 ml (½ pint) stock
1 can brown ale
thickly cut rounds of French bread
made mustard

Cut the meat into small pieces and slice the onions. Mix the flour with the seasoning and coat the meat with the mixture. Melt the fat in a pan and fry the meat with onion until it is brown on both sides. Place in a casserole and add the stock and brown ale. Cover and cook in centre of moderate oven, 180°C (350°F)/Gas 4, for about 2 hours or until the meat is tender.

Remove the lid from the casserole. Spread the bread on the top side with made mustard and place rounds over the top of the beef. Use enough rounds of bread to cover completely the carbonnade. Press with a spoon so that the bread absorbs some of the liquid in the casserole. Return to oven without the lid to cook for a further 20 minutes.

Chicken Mille Feuilles

My husband insists on calling this Chicken Meal, but don't be put off. It doesn't take long to prepare and is quite spectacular in its own way.

225 g (8 oz) frozen puff pastry
50 g (2 oz) butter
50 g (2 oz) flour
250 ml (½ pint) chicken stock
225 g (8 oz) cooked chicken cut into small pieces
100 g (4 oz) ham
2 tablespoons chopped parsley
1 teaspoon mustard
1 teaspoon salt
pinch black pepper

Cut the pastry into three equal portions. Roll out each portion to approximately 23 × 10 cm (9 × 4 in). Lay the pieces on a large baking tray and bake in a pre-heated oven, 200°C (400°F)/Gas 6, for 15 minutes.

While this is cooking, melt the butter in a saucepan. Remove from the heat, stir in the flour and gradually add the chicken stock. Return to the heat and bring to a boil, beating briskly until thick. Beat again to make sure there are no lumps. Add the chicken pieces and chopped ham, parsley and seasoning.

Lay one pastry layer in an ovenproof dish and spread over half the chicken mixture. Place another pastry layer on top and spread with the rest of the mixture. Top with remaining pastry. Return to the oven, now set at 160°C (325°F)/Gas 3, to reheat for 20 minutes.

Chicken Rama

This is a delicious spicy curry that can be made in two easy stages. It is garlicky, as you can see, so choose your time to serve it with a certain amount of discretion.

1 1.35-kg (3-lb) roasting chicken
1 125-ml (5-oz) carton natural yoghurt
1 teaspoon ground turmeric
½ teaspoon chilli powder
1 teaspoon cumin seeds
1 teaspoon coriander
½ teaspoon garlic powder
2 medium-sized onions
6 cloves garlic
4 tablespoons cooking oil
8 cloves
2 bay leaves
1 teaspoon powdered cinnamon or 1 2.5-cm (1-in) stick of cinnamon

Cut the chicken into required number of joints. Make the marinade by mixing the yoghurt with the turmeric, chilli powder, cumin, coriander and garlic powder. Coat the chicken joints and leave as long as possible—up to 12 hours if you can. When you drain them, be sure to reserve the marinade.

Grate the onion and finely chop the garlic. Heat the oil in a pan, brown the onion and garlic, add spices, bay leaves and chicken joints. Brown well, stirring with a wooden spoon to prevent sticking. Add the reserved juice in which chicken was marinated, made up with about 125 ml (¼ pint) water. Stir well, then put a lid on the pan and simmer over a low flame for about 20–25 minutes. Check that the chicken is cooked (the flesh will leave the bone very easily) before serving with plain boiled rice and a chutney such as mango.

Chicken the French Way

This has been a true family favourite from the very first time our charming Breton au pair girl showed me how to prepare it. It's easy and quick, and I have never known anyone who didn't ask for second helpings.

1 chicken, about 1.35 kg (3 lb) in weight
450 g (1 lb) medium-sized potatoes

225 g (½ lb) onions
2 or 3 carrots
100 g (4 oz) butter
salt and pepper

Place the whole chicken in a roasting pan. Slice the potatoes into medium thick slices. Chop the onions finely and dice the carrots. Surround the chicken with the vegetables and season well. Cut butter into pieces and put two knobs on top of the chicken and the rest over the vegetables.

Bake in the top half of the oven at 200°C (400°F)/Gas 6 for 50 minutes to 1 hour. Baste once or twice during cooking.

Do use butter for this and no substitute. It won't taste the same with anything else. As the meal is quite rich, it is best served with a green salad with a French dressing to sharpen the flavour.

Spiced Chicken

This is a mild curry by most people's standards, though one man's sauna may be another man's cold bath, as they say.

2 cloves garlic
4 chicken joints
½ teaspoon cumin seeds
½ teaspoon coriander seeds
7 or 8 cloves
1 piece of fresh root ginger or 1 teaspoon powdered ginger
½ teaspoon powdered cinnamon or a 2.5-cm (1-in) stick
1 teaspoon chilli powder
375 ml (¾ pint) natural yoghurt
oil for frying
2 large onions
1 teaspoon salt
1 teaspoon cornflour

Chop the garlic finely, arrange on top of the chicken joints and set aside. Grind the cumin, coriander and cloves, using a pestle and mortar if you have one or the end of a wooden rolling pin and an ordinary bowl. Add the ginger, cinnamon and chilli powder and mix together. Stir into the yoghurt and pour over the chicken.

Into a heavy saucepan pour the oil and heat gently. Chop the onions coarsely and fry gently in the oil. Add the chicken joints and brown lightly, then pour in the yoghurt. Season with salt. Cook gently over a low flame for 1½ hours, stirring from time to time. The sauce should be thick. If necessary, remove the chicken from the pan, blend a little of the sauce with 1 teaspoon cornflour, add this to the sauce and stir over the heat until it is sufficiently thick. Then replace joints in the pan to coat them in the sauce.

Serve with savoury rice (page 129) and a tomato and pepper salad.

Turkey and Apricot Flan

This is an ideal recipe for using up Christmas leftovers. But it is quite easy to make on other days, and the sweet-sour taste really is very 'moorish'.

For the pastry:
150 g (6 oz) plain flour
37.5 g (1¼ oz) butter
37.5 g (1¼ oz) lard
pinch salt

For the filling:
100 g (4 oz) apricots previously soaked for 3–4 hours
3 tablespoons sage and onion stuffing (page 130)
350 g (12 oz) cooked turkey
25 g (1 oz) butter
25 g (1 oz) flour
250 ml (½ pint) chicken stock
75 g (3 oz) grated Cheddar cheese

Preheat the oven to 190°C (375°F)/Gas 5. Sift the flour and salt into a bowl, and add the fat cut into small pieces. Blend with your fingertips until the mixture resembles fine breadcrumbs, then mix with water to form a firm dough. Roll out and line 20-cm (8-in) flan dish. Prick the base with a fork, fill the centre with greaseproof paper and rice or beans to hold down the pastry. Bake 'blind' for 15 minutes. Remove from the oven and reduce heat to 160°C (325°F)/Gas 3.

Poach the apricots in a small amount of water for 10–15 minutes. Drain and roughly chop them, and arrange them on the bottom of the flan case. Make up the sage and onion stuffing and spread this over the apricots. Top with the flaked turkey and season well.

Melt the butter in a saucepan, remove from heat, and stir in the flour. Add the stock gradually, stirring well to avoid lumps. Reheat, stirring continually until the sauce thickens. Pour over the mixture in the flan case. Put in the oven for 20 minutes. Just before serving, sprinkle grated cheese on top and brown under the grill. Serve at once.

Casserole of Pigeon

Pigeon has a flavour all its own, but needs to be well cooked. Use the times here as a guideline and make sure the flesh is tender before you serve the casserole.

450 g (1 lb) small pickling onions
25 g (1 oz) fat
4 pigeons (cleaned and gutted)
seasoning
1 bay leaf
375 ml (¾ pint) beef stock

For the forcemeat balls:
225 g (8 oz) pork sausage meat
1 thick slice fresh bread (grated after crusts have been removed)
2 tablespoons chopped parsley and thyme mixed
12.5 g (¼ oz) flour
25 g (1 oz) cooking fat

Peel the onions and leave them whole. Melt the fat in a frying pan and fry the onions, shaking them so that they are evenly brown all over. Remove onions and put them at the bottom of a deep casserole. Fry the pigeons on all sides, then place them in the casserole. Season well, add the bay leaf and stock. Bring to a boil, then cover tightly and simmer for 1 hour.

Make the forcemeat stuffing by mixing sausage meat with the grated breadcrumbs and herbs. Roll into 8 even-sized balls. Dust with flour. Melt the fat in a pan and brown the forcemeat balls on all sides. Add them to the casserole when it has been cooking for 1 hour, and simmer for a further 30 minutes. Test to see that the pigeons are cooked by putting a sharp knife between the flesh and the bone; it should come away easily.

Savoury Rabbit

Rabbit needs a bit of dressing up, so don't stint on the herb stuffing.

1 rabbit
3 rashers streaky bacon
flour
2 tablespoons sage and onion stuffing mix
salt and pepper
250 ml (½ pint) stock
225 g (8 oz) pork chipolatas

Cut the rabbit into joints. Trim the rinds from the bacon rashers, cut into chunky strips, and fry gently. Add the rabbit joints after coating them with flour and fry until just brown. Place in a casserole, sprinkle with the sage and onion stuffing and season with salt and pepper. Add stock. Place in moderate oven, 160°C (325°F)/Gas 3, for 1½ hours.

Brown the sausages and cook them gently. At the end of 1½ hours, add them to the stew and return to oven for an extra ½ hour.

Casserole of Hare

One hare is a generous serving for six people, so you can use some of the meat to make a terrine of hare (page 111).

1 large hare
125 ml (¼ pint) red wine
8 or 9 peppercorns
½ teaspoon salt
2 bay leaves
50 g (2 oz) flour
2 tablespoons oil
250 ml (½ pint) stock

Ask the butcher to cut the hare into suitable joints. Put the wine, peppercorns, salt and bay leaves into a dish and add the hare joints. Coat them in the liquid and leave them in this marinade for 24 hours, turning the joints from time to time.

Remove joints from the marinade, dry on kitchen paper and coat with flour. In a heavy ovenproof pan heat the oil and sauté the hare until brown on both sides. Pour over the marinade liquid and the stock. Transfer the pan to the oven and cook at 180°C (350°F)/Gas 4 for two hours.

Stuffed Hearts

Don't despise hearts—they're very tasty served this way. Roast potatoes and braised red cabbage make good accompaniments.

4 lamb's hearts
1 teaspoon salt

For the stuffing:
225 g (8 oz) pork sausage meat
50 g (2 oz) fresh breadcrumbs
1 tablespoon parsley
salt and pepper
125 ml (¼ pint) beef stock

Wash the hearts well and remove the inside tubes with a sharp knife, so that one single cavity remains. Soak them for an hour or more in cold salted water. Drain thoroughly.

Make the stuffing by mixing the sausage meat with the breadcrumbs, parsley and seasoning. Put one quarter of the mixture in each heart. Place in an ovenproof dish and pour over the stock. Cover with a tight fitting lid and cook for 1 hour at 180°C (350°F)/Gas 4. Baste the hearts with the liquid once or twice during the cooking.

Devilled Kidneys

8 lamb's kidneys
1 level tablespoon flour
1 level tablespoon mustard
1 teaspoon curry powder
50 g (2 oz) butter
125 ml (¼ pint) beef stock
1 tablespoon mango chutney
salt and pepper

Put the kidneys in cold water over a high heat. As soon as they have come to a boil, discard liquid and rinse kidneys in cold water. Skin and core by removing the white. Cut into slices. Mix together the flour, mustard and curry powder. Coat the kidney slices. Melt the butter in a pan and fry kidneys gently. Add beef stock and mango chutney, and season well. Cover the pan with a lid and simmer for 20 minutes. Check to see the liquid doesn't run dry and add a little extra stock or water if necessary.

Serve with plain boiled rice or noodles.

Braised Lamb's Liver

sage and onion stuffing (page 130)
2 medium-sized onions
1 tablespoon flour
450 g (1 lb) lamb's liver (sliced)
250 ml (½ pint) stock
seasoning

Make up the sage and onion stuffing. Chop the onions finely. Lightly flour the liver slices and place in a baking tin with the chopped onion. Put a portion of stuffing on each piece of liver, pour over the stock and season. Cover with foil or a lid and bake in the oven at 190°C (375°F)/Gas 5 for about 45 minutes.

Serve with jacket potatoes, carrots and red or white cabbage.

Oxtail Stew

1 oxtail
1 tablespoon oil
2 medium-sized onions
2 bay leaves (optional)
375 ml (¾ pint) stock
1 teaspoon salt
pepper

1 dessertspoon curry powder
1 small swede (about 225 g (8 oz))
225 g (8 oz) carrots
small turnip

Cut the oxtail into pieces. Heat the oil and fry the meat, adding finely chopped onion. When the meat is brown all over and the onions are soft add bay leaves, stock, seasoning and curry powder. Cook in centre of the oven, 180°C (350°F)/Gas 4, for 2 hours. Skim off the fat. This is most easily done if the casserole is allowed to cool, after which the fat can be lifted from the top.

Cut the swede, carrots and turnip into small pieces, add to casserole and continue cooking for another 2 hours.

Whiting in Hiding

Homely fish like whiting have now come into their own since fish prices have soared. Try this mild curry recipe and keep the family guessing.

550 g (1¼ lb) whiting
225 g (½ lb) mashed potato (or 1 packet instant potato made up with 375 ml (¾ pint) water)
1 thick slice white bread
1 teaspoon curry powder
seasoning
1 egg
50 g (2 oz) flour
2 tablespoons vegetable oil

For the curry sauce:
25 g (1 oz) butter
25 g (1 oz) flour
1 teaspoon curry powder
1 teaspoon powdered ginger
½ pint fish stock retained after cooking whiting
1 tablespoon brown sugar
50 g (2 oz) sultanas

Poach the whiting gently in a little water until cooked—about 10–15 minutes. Retain 250 ml (½ pint) water as fish stock. Remove bones from fish and flake into small pieces with a fork. Prepare 225 g (½ lb) cooked mashed potato or make up instant potato as directed on the packet. Grate bread into crumbs. Mix all together until well blended. Add curry powder and seasoning. Beat the egg and add to mixture to bind. Form into 8 flat cakes, coat with flour and fry in oil until brown on both sides. Keep hot.

To make sauce, melt the butter, remove from heat, stir in flour, ginger and curry powder. Gradually stir in the fish stock. Return to heat and stir rapidly until boiling. Continue to cook for two minutes, stirring well. Add brown sugar and sultanas. Pour over fish cakes and serve with savoury rice (page 129).

Plaice with Mushroom Stuffing

An attractive variation to plain fish, and quick and easy to prepare.

4 small whole plaice
25 g (1 oz) butter
50 g (2 oz) mushrooms
50 g (2 oz) breadcrumbs
1 stick celery
rind and juice of 1 lemon

Ask your fishmonger to clean and trim the plaice. Wash them well and place them on a board with the white sides uppermost. Use a sharp knife and make a slit down the backbone of each fish, then ease the flesh away from each side so that a small 'pocket' is formed.

Melt the butter in a pan, fry the mushrooms gently then add the breadcrumbs, chopped celery and grated rind and juice of the lemon. Cook for a little longer. Put one quarter of this stuffing into the 'pocket' you have made in each plaice. Place the fish in a large baking pan, cover with foil or buttered greaseproof paper and cook at 200°C (400°F)/Gas 6 for 20 minutes.

Cod in the Corn

Cod is a luxury now so you could use portions of coley instead.

1 small onion
1 stick celery
2 tablespoons sweet corn
1 slice fresh bread (grated and crusts removed)
seasoning
1 egg yolk
4 cod cutlets
50 g (2 oz) butter

To prepare the topping finely chop the onion and celery. Add the sweet corn, and breadcrumbs, season well and bind with an egg yolk. Spread the mixture equally over the cod steaks, top each with a knob of butter, cover with greased, greaseproof paper and bake in a moderate oven, 180°C (350°F)/Gas 4, for 35–50 minutes.

Savoury Pancake Layers with Lamb

Make the pancakes in advance and the meal is quite quickly prepared.

For the pancakes:
100 g (4 oz) flour
pinch salt
1 egg
1 teaspoon oil
250 ml (¼ pint) milk and water mixed
1 tablespoon oil for cooking pancakes

For the filling:
50 g (2 oz) butter
1 green pepper
100 g (4 oz) mushrooms
1 tablespoon tomato purée
450 g (1 lb) cooked lamb (cut into small pieces)
25 g (1 oz) flour
250 ml (¼ pint) chicken stock

To make the pancakes, sieve the flour and salt into a bowl. Stand the bowl on a damp sponge to stop it moving about. Make a well in the centre of flour and break the egg into it. Add 1 teaspoon oil. Gradually beat with a wooden spoon to draw in the flour. Mix in milk and water gradually, making a smooth batter. If it should become lumpy just whisk the batter with a fork or balloon whisk if you have one.

Wipe a small heavy-based frying pan with salt and kitchen paper. Warm the pan gently over a low heat. Pour in a tablespoon of oil to coat the pan. Heat gently, then pour the oil into a cup and stand it on one side. Pour in enough batter to *just* coat the bottom of the pan very thinly. Move the pan so that the batter heats evenly. Turn the pancake over with a spatula or kitchen slice and cook the other side. Repeat until you have used all the batter. Keep the cooked pancakes warm on a plate resting over a saucepan of hot water. Aim to make about 8–10 pancakes out of this mixture—it will depend on the size of the pan you are using. Being thoroughly childish at heart I usually play a game with myself to see how little batter I can use to coat the base of the pan.

To make the filling, heat 25 g (1 oz) of the butter and fry the green pepper which has been deseeded and chopped into small pieces. Add the chopped mushrooms, cook for a few minutes and then add the tomato purée and the lamb. Cover the pan and heat gently.

In a separate pan, melt the remaining 25 g (1 oz) butter. Remove from heat. Stir in the flour, then gradually add stock. Return to heat, stirring until boiling point is reached. Remove from heat.

To assemble, place one pancake at the bottom of an ovenproof dish (a flan dish is ideal). Put a little of the lamb mixture on top, spreading it well out around the edges. Add another pancake, then more filling, and so on, ending with a pancake.

Pour over sauce, cover with foil and place in a moderate oven, 180°C (350°F)/Gas 4 for 20 minutes. Serve in wedges, like cake.

Savoury Rice

1 tablespoon oil
1 medium-sized onion
225 g (8 oz) long grain rice
500 ml (1 pint) chicken stock
2 tablespoons green peas
1 small can sweetcorn with pepper

Heat the oil in a medium-sized saucepan. Chop and gently fry the onion in the oil until soft. Add the rice and fry gently for a few more minutes. Pour in the stock and stir to prevent rice sticking. Bring to a boil, reduce heat, and simmer for 20 minutes, stirring from time to time. By this time the rice should have absorbed the stock. Add the peas and sweetcorn with pepper, warm through, and serve.

Savoury Cabbage Basket

This makes an inexpensive and unusual supper dish. As the cabbage needs to be quite firm, it is not particularly suitable to serve to elderly people.

1 white cabbage, about 1 kg (2¼ lb) in weight
2 medium-sized onions
25 g (1 oz) lard
350 g (12 oz) minced beef
1 green pepper
2 sticks celery
1 teaspoon tomato purée
seasoning
1 teaspoon Worcestershire sauce
1 tablespoon Branston pickle

Sharply trim off the bottom stalk of cabbage so that it rests flat. Using a sharp knife, cut a hollow out of the top of the cabbage so that you are left with a shell about 2.5 cm (1 in) thick. Do this very carefully to retain the shell in one piece. Use a spoon to remove as much cabbage as possible from the inside. Set the cabbage pieces aside and tie a string round the shell.

Bring a sufficiently large pan of water to the boil and put whole cabbage into it. Allow to simmer for about 7–8 minutes. Remove, drain well.

Meanwhile, make the filling. Chop the onions and fry them in the lard. Add the minced beef, chopped green pepper, and celery chopped into small pieces. Continue cooking over a gentle heat for five minutes. Season well, stir in tomato purée, Worcestershire sauce and Branston pickle.

Pile the mixture into the cabbage shell. Cover with foil and cook in the centre of the oven at 200°C (400°F)/Gas 6, for one hour. To serve, cut the stuffed cabbage in wedges like a cake. The remaining cabbage shreds can be served at the same time if you wish, or saved for another meal.

Spiced Red Cabbage

1 medium-sized red cabbage—about 900 g (2 lb)
450 g (1 lb) cooking apples
2 medium-sized onions
salt and pepper
100 g (4 oz) brown sugar
250 ml (½ pint) stock
1 tablespoon vinegar

Shred the cabbage coarsely. Peel, core and chop the apples into thin slices. Chop the onions finely.

Place one good layer of red cabbage into the bottom of an ovenproof casserole. Put a thin layer of apple on top, followed by a layer of onion. Season and sprinkle with sugar. Repeat the layers then pour over the stock and vinegar. Cover tightly and cook in the oven, 160°C (325°F)/Gas 3, for 1½ hours. Serve with hare, pork, sausages or frankfurters.
Serves 6–8

Sage and Onion Stuffing

2 medium-sized onions
100 g (4 oz) fresh breadcrumbs
25 g (1 oz) shredded suet
2 tablespoons chopped fresh sage (or 1 tablespoon dried)
salt and pepper
1 small egg

Peel the onions, put them in a saucepan of cold water, bring to a boil and simmer for 2–3 minutes. Drain, cool and finely chop. Mix together the breadcrumbs, suet, chopped onions and sage. Season well and bind with the beaten egg. Use as directed in the recipes.

Desserts

Baked Bananas

Allow 1½ bananas per person.

6 large bananas
juice of 1 lemon
50 g (2 oz) butter
3 tablespoons brown sugar
1 teaspoon mixed spice

Peel the bananas, cut in two lengthwise and put in a shallow ovenproof dish. Sprinkle over the lemon juice. Put knobs of butter evenly over bananas, then sprinkle with mixed sugar and spice. Cover with buttered paper and bake at 190°C (375°F)/Gas 5 for 15 minutes. Serve with cream.

Prune and Almond Lattice Tart

For the pastry:
200 g (8 oz) plain flour
1 teaspoon salt
50 g (2 oz) lard
50 g (2 oz) butter

For the filling:
100 g (4 oz) butter
100 g (4 oz) caster sugar
¼ teaspoon almond essence
2 standard eggs
50 g (2 oz) ground almonds
50 g (2 oz) semolina
225 g (8 oz) prunes soaked overnight in cold tea
little milk

Sieve the flour and salt into a bowl. Cut the fat into small pieces and rub it in with your fingertips until the mixture resembles fine breadcrumbs. Add cold water and mix with your fingers or a spatula until well blended. Roll out to fill a 20-cm (8-in) flan case.

Preheat the oven to 180°C (350°F)/Gas 4. Simmer prunes for about 10 minutes in the liquid in which they have been standing. Remove stones carefully so that the fruit is still whole. Soften the butter by beating well, then add sugar and continue beating until it is soft and fluffy and has lost its grainy texture. Add the almond essence, beat in the eggs one at a time, then stir in the ground almonds and semolina. Spread over the pastry base. Place the prunes in straight lines over the almond mixture. Use the remaining scraps of pastry to make a lattice over the top. Seal the pastry strips to the edge with water. Brush the pastry with milk and cook in the oven, for 40–50 minutes.

Marmalade Apple Tart

The deliciously tart flavour of the filling makes a pleasing contrast to the sweet pastry.

For the rich shortcrust pastry:
200 g (8 oz) plain flour
100 g (4 oz) butter
25 g (1 oz) caster sugar
1 egg yolk
½ teaspoon salt
cold water to mix

For the filling:
25 g (1 oz) butter
1 kg (2¼ lb) cooking apples
½ lemon
2 tablespoons marmalade

To make the pastry, sift the flour and salt into a bowl. Cut the butter into pieces and rub in to the flour until the mixture resembles fine breadcrumbs. Add sugar, then the egg yolk and enough cold water to mix to a firm dough. Roll out and use three-quarters of the dough to line a 20-cm (8-in) flan case.

Melt the butter in a heavy-based pan. Cut the apples into four, but do not peel or core them. Add the rind and juice of half a lemon, cover the pan tightly and cook very gently until the apples are mushy. Stir from time to time to prevent apples sticking. Press through a sieve or use the fine sieve on a Mouli if you have one.

Spread the marmalade in the bottom of the flan and pour over the apple purée. Sweeten if you wish, but the real charm of this recipe is the tartness of the apple contrasting with the sweet pastry. Roll out the rest of the pastry in strips and form a lattice over the tart. Bake at 190°C (375°F)/Gas 5 for 30 minutes.

Apple Cheese Tart

Cheese pastry is unusual, and very good done this way with apple purée. Do sweeten to taste, as some people might find the flavour rather tart.

132

For the pastry:
150 g (6 oz) cream cheese
150 g (6 oz) butter
150 g (6 oz) wholemeal flour

For the filling:
450 g (1 lb) cooking apples
25 g (1 oz) butter
1 tablespoon water
rind and juice of ½ lemon
12 ground cloves
50 g (2 oz) caster sugar

To make the pastry, beat the cream cheese and butter together and when well blended beat in the flour. Allow the mixture to chill a little.

For the apple purée, cut and core but don't peel the apples. Put the butter and water at the bottom of the pan and then add the apples. Cover with a tight-fitting lid and cook over a low heat until the apples are really soft. Shake the pan from time to time and check to ensure they don't stick to the bottom. Sieve through a Mouli if you have one, or if not press through a sieve using the back of a wooden spoon. Add grated rind and lemon juice, the ground cloves and the sugar.

Preheat the oven to 180°C (350°F)/Gas 4. Roll out and press the pastry around the sides and bottom of a 20-cm (8-in) flan dish. It is crumbly at this stage, but press together as necessary. Pour in the apple purée and cook in the oven for 40 minutes. Serve with plenty of cream.

Almond Cake

This is a no-flour basic cake that can combine with many different fillings to provide delicious gâteaux for desserts.

3 eggs
100 g (4 oz) caster sugar
rind and juice of ½ lemon
75 g (3 oz) semolina
25 g (1 oz) ground almonds

Preheat the oven to 180°C (350°F)/Gas 4. Prepare sandwich tins by greasing them well, then sprinkling them with flour. Shake off any excess flour. Separate the eggs. Whisk yolks and caster sugar together until white and creamy and thick enough to leave a trail. Add the rind and juice of the lemon, the semolina and the ground almonds. Whisk the whites until stiff, then fold them into the mixture with a metal spoon. Divide into two 17.5-cm (7-in) sandwich tins and bake for 20 minutes. Leave to cool in the tin.

Any number of fillings can be made for this cake, depending on how you wish to serve it. A few suggestions follow, but experiment using the various fruits in season.

Chop 2 pears which you have poached in vanilla-flavoured sugar syrup, drain and fold into whipped double cream (use half of a 125-ml (¼-pint) carton). Sandwich the cake together, then cover with more cream.

Use about 100 g (4 oz) green and black grapes mixed, de-seeded and folded into 125 ml (¼ pint) whipped double cream, sweetened with a little caster sugar. Decorate the top with cream and grapes halved lengthwise, alternating the green and black colours.

Slice 2 bananas, sprinkle them with lemon juice and combine with 2–3 tablespoons apricot purée or jam as a filling. Whip 2 tablespoons cream and decorate the top of the cake with the cream and remaining banana slices.

In the summer, use crushed raspberries or blackcurrants.

Pear Upside-down Cake

A very substantial sweet that is usually a firm favourite with the men.

For the topping:
2 firm pears (Conference are ideal)
50 g (2 oz) butter
25 g (1 oz) caster sugar
two or three glacé cherries to decorate

For the gingerbread:
100 g (4 oz) butter
150 g (6 oz) black treacle
50 g (2 oz) soft brown sugar
125 ml (¼ pint) milk
2 eggs
225 g (8 oz) plain flour
2 teaspoons mixed spice
1 teaspoon ground ginger
1 teaspoon bicarbonate of soda

Preheat oven to 150°C (300°F)/Gas 2. Thoroughly grease a 17.5-cm (7-in) deep cake tin. Peel, core and slice the pears and arrange them cut side up around the bottom of the tin. Cream together the sugar and butter for the topping and dot evenly over the pears.

To make the gingerbread, put the butter, treacle and brown sugar in a saucepan and heat gently until butter has melted. Stir. Add the milk, and allow to cool slightly before adding the eggs, which have been beaten until the yolks and whites are blended. Sift flour, spices and soda into a bowl and pour in the treacle mixture gradually, beating well to achieve a smooth consistency. Pour this over the pears and bake in the oven for 1–1¼ hours. Allow the cake to shrink from the sides of the tin before turning out; cut glacé cherries in half and arrange amongst the pears before serving.

Chocolate with Orange Gateau

This is a sweet for when you're 'pushing the boat out'. You can omit the Cointreau, but it won't taste as good.

For the sponge:
3 standard eggs
75 g (3 oz) caster sugar
50 g (2 oz) flour
25 g (1 oz) cocoa

For the filling:
50 g (2 oz) granulated sugar
125 ml (¼ pint) water
2 tablespoons Cointreau
3 large oranges
1 125-ml (5-oz) carton double cream
1 tablespoon caster sugar

Preheat the oven to 180°C (350°F)/Gas 4. Prepare two 17.5-cm (7-in) sandwich tins by greasing them and lightly sprinkling over with flour.

Break the eggs into a bowl, add caster sugar and whisk over hot water until the mixture is thick and creamy and leaves a trail. If you have an electric mixer you can whisk it without standing it over hot water.

Add the flour and cocoa, mixed; fold in very lightly using a metal spoon. Divide equally into the two sandwich tins and bake immediately (the mixture will sink if you delay) for 20 minutes. Remove from oven and leave to cool in the tin until the cake has shrunk away from the sides. Turn on to a cake rack to finish cooling.

To prepare the filling, heat the granulated sugar and water gently until sugar has dissolved, then boil fast for a few minutes. Allow the syrup to cool then add 1 tablespoon Cointreau. Stand each cake on a plate, pierce with a fork and spoon over the syrup to moisten. Allow to stand. Peel the oranges so that all the pith is removed, then cut them into slices. Lay them in a dish and sprinkle over the remaining tablespoon of Cointreau. Let the orange slices marinate in this juice for at least 1 hour. Use any liquid in the oranges to spoon over the sponge cakes before spreading the cream.

Whip cream and add caster sugar to sweeten. Put half the oranges on one sponge cake spread with whipped cream, then top with the other sponge. Spread with remaining cream and arrange orange slices on top.

Marmalade Sponge

A warming sweet just right for a cold evening.

225 g (8 oz) plain flour
½ teaspoon salt
2 level teaspoons baking powder
85 g (3 oz) butter
1 egg made up to 125 ml (¼ pint) with milk
1 tablespoon thick cut marmalade

For the sauce:
4 tablespoons marmalade
2 tablespoons water

Sieve the flour, salt and baking powder into a bowl. Cut the butter into pieces and mix into the flour until the mixture resembles fine breadcrumbs. Beat the egg in a measuring jug or bowl and make up to 125 ml (¼ pint) with milk. Blend the milk into the flour with the marmalade and beat well until smooth.

Put the mixture into a greased 750-ml (1½-pint) pudding basin, so that the basin is no more than two-thirds full. Cover with foil or greaseproof paper and a pudding basin cover. Put into a saucepan of cold water so that the water is about halfway up the basin. Bring slowly to the boil, then turn down the heat and let the pudding simmer gently for 1½ hours.

Turn out on to a plate. Heat the marmalade and water in a pan until bubbling, and serve separately as a sauce.

Lemon Sponge with Lemon Sauce

75 g (3 oz) butter
75 g (3 oz) caster sugar
grated rind of 1 lemon
1 beaten egg made up to 100 ml (4 fl oz) with milk
150 g (6 oz) self-raising flour

For the sauce:
2 lemons (include the one from which lemon rind has been grated)
1 teaspoon cornflour
2 tablespoons caster sugar

Grease a pudding basin. Cream together butter and sugar until light and fluffy. Add lemon rind, then egg mixture and flour alternately, a little at a time, beating well. The mixture should be soft but quite stiff. Turn into basin, cover with foil. Put in a pan and surround two thirds of the way up with cold water. Bring to a boil and simmer gently for 1¼ hours.

To make the sauce, grate rind from remaining lemon. Squeeze juice from both lemons and make up to 125 ml (¼ pint) with water. Blend cornflour and sugar and take a little of the liquid to blend to a smooth paste. Bring remaining liquid to the boil and pour on to cornflour paste, stirring well. Return to pan and simmer stirring constantly until thickened.

Turn pudding out on to a plate and serve the hot lemon sauce separately.

Hazelnut Meringue

Read the instructions for making meringue carefully and you'll have no trouble with this eye-catching, three-layer sweet.

whites of 3 standard eggs
150 g (6 oz) caster sugar
100 g (4 oz) hazelnuts
1 125-ml (5-oz) carton double cream
1 teaspoon vanilla essence

Meringue is not difficult to make if a few basic rules are observed. Eggs should not be too new. All utensils must be clean, dry and free from grease. Sugar must be added carefully and the drying out must be done very, very slowly.

Whisk the egg whites until they are stiff and will stand in peaks. Add one-third of the sugar and continue whisking until the mixture peaks again. Add half the remaining sugar and whisk again. At this stage the meringue mixture looses its cotton wool appearance and becomes closer in texture. Sprinkle the last of the sugar on top and whisk only long enough for it to be absorbed.

Oil 3 sheets of greaseproof paper and spread the mixture into three equal rounds, one on each sheet. You can pipe the meringue if you wish but perfectly good results can be achieved by using the back of a spoon. Put the meringues on 3 baking sheets and sprinkle a little more sugar over them. Dry the shells in a very low oven, 120°C (250°F)/Gas ½, for about two hours. Remove from the oven and carefully peel off the greaseproof paper. Turn the shells upside down and return them to the oven with the heat turned off to dry them out even further. These can be kept in an airtight tin for a week or two.

To assemble the gâteau, bake the hazelnuts in the oven or grill them for a few minutes to toast them. Rub off the skins, then chop nuts coarsely. Whip the cream and add vanilla essence. Spread one meringue shell with one-third of the cream and scatter one-third of the hazelnuts on top. Repeat with the next two meringue shells, finishing with a final layer of cream and nuts.

Cut with a very sharp knife and serve in wedges.

Apricot Meringue Pudding

This is a jazzed-up version of the homely bread and butter pudding. It looks good and you can serve it to guests without a qualm.

100 g (4 oz) dried apricots
6 slices buttered bread with crusts removed
50 g (2 oz) caster sugar
2 eggs
250 ml (½ pint) milk

Soak the apricots in water overnight. Next day, grease a deep pie dish and put two slices of bread, butter side up, at the bottom. Arrange half the apricot slices on the bread and sprinkle with a little of the sugar. Then add another layer of bread, the rest of the apricot slices, a little sugar and the rest of the bread. Be sure to retain half the original amount of sugar to fold into the meringue.

Separate the eggs. Heat the milk until just warm, beat in the egg yolks and pour over the bread. Whip the egg whites until stiff, fold in the remaining sugar with a metal spoon and pile over the top of the dish.

Cook at 190°C (375°F)/Gas 5 for 15 minutes and serve at once. Do not allow the meringue to become too brown. If in doubt, cover with a piece of foil.

Rhubarb Cream

This sweet is a fairly liquid consistency and is best served in glasses and eaten with a small spoon.

450 g (1 lb) rhubarb
rind and juice of 1 small lemon
3 tablespoons water
75 g (3 oz) brown sugar
½ teaspoon powdered cinnamon
2 eggs
1 125-ml (5-oz) carton of sour cream

Cut the rhubarb into small pieces and put them in a saucepan. Add the grated rind and juice of the lemon. (It's well worth putting the whole lemon in hot water for a few minutes before squeezing it to extract maximum juice.) Add 3 tablespoons water with the sugar and cinnamon, then simmer gently until rhubarb is soft. Sieve or whisk in a blender. Separate the whites from the yolks of the eggs. When the rhubarb purée is sufficiently cool, add egg yolks and sour cream and beat in well. Whisk the egg whites until stiff, then fold into the mixture. Chill until ready to serve.

Banana Marshmallow Cream

Marshmallows and bananas—a gorgeously, sinfully rich combination. Try it and see!

250 ml (½ pint) milk
¼ teaspoon vanilla essence
20 g (¾ oz) sugar
20 g (¾ oz) cornflour
1 125-ml (5-oz) carton double cream
12 marshmallows
2 ripe bananas
8 Barmouth or similar plain biscuits

Heat the milk, vanilla essence and sugar. Mix the cornflour to a smooth paste with a little of the milk from the pan. Bring remainder to a rising boil, then stir briskly on to the cornflour until it is smooth. Return to the pan and stir until thick. Put the mixture into a container, cover with wet greaseproof paper to prevent skin forming and leave to cool.

Whisk the cream until stiff, then fold into the custard and whisk until blended and smooth.

Snip six of the marshmallows (use wet scissors to make it easy) and put the pieces at the bottom of a straight-sided serving dish. Slice the bananas and put them over the marshmallows. Pour in the custard mixture, smooth the top and put the biscuits around the edge. Chill. Just before serving, arrange the remaining marshmallows in a pattern on the top.

Winter Fruit Fool

This can only be made satisfactorily if you have a liquidiser.

225 g (8 oz) dried apricots soaked in water overnight
3 ripe bananas
1 125-ml (5-oz) carton double cream
1 tablespoon milk
1 tablespoon marmalade
1 tablespoon clear honey
angelica for decoration

Drain the apricots. Peel the bananas and cut them into small pieces. Place all the ingredients in a blender and switch on low, then increase speed to medium and blend for a minute or so until the mixture is smooth.

If the mixture seems a little thick, add another tablespoon of milk. Spoon into glasses and chill. Just before serving, decorate with diamonds of angelica.

Prune Soufflé

Purists will be aghast at the suggestion that a soufflé can look very nice in a glass dish or china fruit bowl. But it saves the worry of putting greased bands round soufflé dishes, wondering whether the mixture will rise above the top and so on. If you do use an unconventional dish, however, pay extra attention to decorating the top.

225 g (8 oz) prunes
3 eggs
75 g (3 oz) caster sugar
12.5 ml ($\frac{1}{2}$ oz) gelatine
1 125-ml (5-oz) carton double cream
8 walnut halves

Soak the prunes overnight in cold water or tea. Next day simmer them gently in the same liquid until they are tender—about 10 minutes. Remove the stones and blend prunes with the liquid in which they have been cooked, to make a thick purée. If you don't have a blender, press the fruit through a sieve by using the back of a wooden spoon.

Separate the egg yolks from the whites. To the egg yolks add the sugar and whisk with an electric mixer until mixture goes creamy and leaves a trail. Alternatively, use a balloon whisk and stand the mixture in a basin over (but not touching) hot water while you whisk. It will take longer, but you will probably find that the volume and texture are better.

Stir in the purée. Put 4 tablespoons water in a cup and sprinkle the gelatine over the top. Stand the cup in a saucepan of hot water and heat slowly until gelatine has melted. Remove from heat, allow to cool a little, then gradually add to the mixture, stirring all the time. Whisk the double cream until it is the same consistency as the egg and purée combination, then stir in about half the cream. Whisk the egg whites until stiff (they will form peaks), and fold them into the mixture with a metal spoon. Use a light touch and don't stir more than necessary. Turn into a glass or china dish and allow to set.

Before serving, spread the remaining cream over the top and decorate with walnut halves.

Glacé Winter Rice

This is a jazzed-up rice pudding—served cold. It is very nice indeed, so don't be frightened to serve it when guests come.

50 g (2 oz) rice
500 ml (1 pint) milk
50 g (2 oz) caster sugar

vanilla pod or 1 teaspoon vanilla essence
12.5 g (½ oz) chopped almonds
25 g (1 oz) chopped glacé cherries
2 pieces angelica (chopped)
2 tablespoons whipped double cream

Put the rice in a pan with a little of the milk and bring to a boil to soften it.
Add the sugar, vanilla pod or essence and rest of milk. Return to the boil,
then turn the heat right down and cook very gently for about 1¼ hours.
Stir the rice from time to time. The object is to make the rice pudding very
soft and creamy. Remove the vanilla pod, leave the rice to cool a little, then
stir in the chopped almonds, glacé cherries and angelica. Lastly fold in the
double cream.

   Oil a 17.5-cm (7-in) ring mould and turn the rice into this. Smooth
round the top. Leave to chill thoroughly. Just before serving turn out on
to a dish. It can be served as it is with more cream, or you can make a
raspberry or blackcurrant sauce by using two or three tablespoons jam
mixed with lemon juice.

Orange Foam

This looks very effective served individually in wine glasses.

3 large eggs
50 g (2 oz) sugar
2 medium-sized oranges
12.5 g (½ oz) gelatine
2 or 3 tablespoons whipped cream

Whisk the eggs and sugar together with the grated rind of both oranges
until thick and foamy. If you have a large mixer this will do the job for
you, otherwise whisk with the bowl over a pan of hot water on a gentle
heat. Extract the juice from the oranges and make up to 200 ml (7 fl oz)
with water. Put the liquid in a mug, sprinkle the gelatine over and stand
the mug in a saucepan of hot water. Heat gently until the gelatine is
dissolved. Cool, pour into orange foam and stir to distribute gelatine.
Leave to cool and just as it is beginning to thicken fold in the whipped
cream. Turn into a dish or individual wine glasses and leave to set.

Malt Ice Cream

If you wish, you can serve this chilled, but not frozen, as a mousse.

1 large can evaporated milk
50 g (2 oz) caster sugar

3 thick slices sticky malt loaf
1 egg white

Boil the unopened can of milk in water for 10 minutes. Remove, cool, then chill thoroughly. Turn the freezer compartment of your refrigerator to its coldest setting.

Whisk the milk hard with the sugar, using an electric mixer if you have one, until the mixture has trebled in bulk and is very thick and creamy. Pour into two ice trays or a plastic container and chill in the freezer compartment. Toast the malt loaf under the grill until it has dried, or put the slices in the oven if you have it on. Crush the slices with a rolling pin; if they are still sticky cut them into small pieces with a sharp knife.

Remove the cream from the fridge and whisk again until slushy. Add the malt crumbs and whisk until blended. Whisk the egg white until stiff, fold into the ice cream gently, then pour back into trays and freeze until firm. Remove to the top of the main refrigerator about an hour before serving.

Calypso Ice Cream

Follow the instructions for malt ice cream but substitute 50 g (2 oz) raisins and 50 g (2 oz) desiccated coconut for the malt loaf.

Luxury Pancakes

Make the pancakes in advance if you wish and store them with a layer of greaseproof paper between each one.

100 g (4 oz) plain flour
pinch salt
1 egg
1 teaspoon oil
250 ml (½ pint) milk

Sift the flour and salt into a bowl. Make a well in centre and break the egg into it. Add the oil. Gradually incorporate the flour from around the sides by beating hard with a wooden spoon. Slowly add the milk, beating until the batter is smooth and has no lumps. Allow the batter to stand for 10 minutes or so.

Heat the pancake pan, and pour in a little oil or butter to coat the surface. Discard any surplus fat, then pour in just enough batter to cover the bottom of the pan. Cook quickly, turn, and cook on the other side. Keep the pancakes hot by putting them on a covered plate over a basin of hot water.

Fillings: Whichever filling you choose, put a little on each pancake, roll up and put in a shallow heatproof dish. Dredge with icing sugar, brown quickly under a grill and serve at once.

Mashed banana sprinkled with lemon juice with redcurrant jelly.

De-pipped grapes with blackcurrant jelly.

Apple purée with grilled flaked almonds. Chop the almonds and brown them under the grill, then add to thick apple purée.

Apricot purée made by stewing dried apricots and pressing them through a sieve. Sweeten to taste and add chopped walnuts.

Cream cheese with sultanas and grated orange rind.

Brandy Snaps

Tell your guests to eat these with their fingers—it's by far the easiest way.

75 g (3 oz) black treacle
75 g (3 oz) soft brown sugar
75 g (3 oz) butter
75 g (3 oz) plain flour
1 teaspoon ground ginger
1 teaspoon grated lemon rind

For the filling:
1 125-ml (¼-pint) carton double cream
1 teaspoon vanilla essence
25 g (1 oz) caster sugar

Preheat the oven to 160°C (325°F)/Gas 3. Place the treacle, sugar and butter in a saucepan and heat gently until the butter and sugar have melted. Cool slightly. Sift the flour and ginger into the mixture with the lemon rind and beat until smooth.

Grease a baking sheet very thoroughly, then put dessertspoons of the mixture on it, leaving a good space between each one. Bake for 7–8 minutes. Leave to cool just a little, then remove from the tin with a sharp palette knife and while still warm roll each biscuit round the handle of a wooden spoon. If the biscuits become brittle before you can finish, return them to the oven for a minute.

Whip the cream with the vanilla essence and caster sugar. When cool, fill each brandy snap with a little cream.

To make a more substantial dessert, sweeten some apple purée, pile it into 4 wine glasses, and top each glass with one or two brandy snaps. Put them in at the last minute before serving or they may go soggy.

PRESERVES

Jams, chutneys and jellies are a wonderfully easy way of using up garden leftovers. Without sounding too prissy, I hope, it really gives a sense of satisfaction to see jars of homemade this and that lining the larder shelves. You'll find they are always well received as unexpected gifts or as contributions to the local bazaar or tombola stand. Of course the best reason of all for spending some time making these condiments is that they taste marvellous.

If you're going into jam-making in any quantities it's well worth buying a sugar thermometer. It takes the guess work out of the whole operation. I bless the day I bought a proper preserving pan too, as before that my jam-making sessions took twice as long as they should have done because I was always trying to boil everything up in too small a pan. Other than this you need a long-handled wooden spoon and a jelly bag or some kind of muslin if you are going to make jellies.

Jam: The aim is to make jam that will set well, keep well and look attractive in colour.

Choose fruit which is just ripe. Damaged parts can be removed and the fruit should be dry and not mouldy.

The setting quality is conditional on the amount of pectin in the fruit. If the fruit is light in pectin, lemon juice or various commercial products can be added. The recipes in the following pages allow for this. To test for setting: If you have a sugar thermometer boil jam until thermometer reaches 104°C (220°F). Another way is to put a teaspoon of jam on a cold saucer and allow it to cool; the jam will wrinkle if it is prodded gently with your finger. Remove jam from the heat while testing.

Jam should be poured into warm dry jars—heat them very gently in the oven or the warming tray if you have one. If there is whole fruit in the jam allow it to cool a little before potting or all the fruit will rise to the top.

Fill the jars to the brim. Either cover immediately with a wax circle or wait until the jam is quite cold. Do *not* cover when the jam is only warm. If you wait until the jam is cold, use Cellophane discs and rubber bands to cover. I usually seal over the wax disc with candle wax from leftover candle stubs, but this is not strictly necessary. Store in a cool dry place to prevent mould.

Jellies: The same principles of jam-making apply to making jellies. When pouring the pulp into the jelly bag to drip overnight don't be tempted to squeeze the pulp or your jelly will become cloudy.

Chutneys: Fruit and vegetables are blended to a pulp and there is no need to test for setting. The chutney is cooked when the liquid and pulp are completely blended together.

When covering chutneys and pickles the cover must be vinegar-proof and airtight. If you use a metal cover it must be protected from the vinegar by wax or a paper disc. A covering of wax is useful, too, to prevent mould forming.

Marrow and Ginger Jam

In our house we use this jam as an alternative to breakfast marmalade. The crisp flavour of the ginger makes a good early morning taste.

2 kg (4½ lb) prepared marrow
75 g (3 oz) root ginger
2 kg (4½ lb) sugar
rind and juice of 3 lemons

Peel the marrow and take out the centre seeds. Cut it into cubes before weighing. Steam in a colander over boiling water until just tender. Put the cooked marrow in a preserving pan with the root ginger tied in muslin. Sprinkle over the sugar and add the rind and juice of the lemons. Cover with a cloth and leave overnight.

Next day, boil steadily until the marrow is transparent, all the liquid has evaporated and the jam is of an even consistency. This will take about 45 minutes. Pour into clean hot jars, and cover with waxed paper. Allow the jam to become quite cold, then cover with wax and seal.

Carrot Jam

This jam is a gorgeous orange in colour and tastes rather like apricot, at well under half the price.

900 g (2 lb) carrots
1 litre (2 pints) water plus sugar
lemons and optional brandy—see quantities below

Grate the carrots and put them in a saucepan with the water. Bring to the boil and simmer until carrots are soft—about 40 minutes. Blend in a liquidiser, use a Mouli, or press through a sieve using the back of a wooden spoon. Weigh the purée.

To each 450 g (1 lb) purée add 450 g (1 lb) sugar, the rind and juice of 2 lemons, and 2 tablespoons brandy. The brandy can be omitted but the jam will not keep long.

Return the purée to the pan, having added the sugar and lemon rind and juice in the quantities mentioned above. Heat until the sugar has dissolved, then boil rapidly until thick and any liquid has been absorbed. Remove from heat, add brandy and stir in well.

Pour at once into warmed jars and leave until cold before sealing.

Orange Rhubarb and Fig Jam

A very sticky jam but delicious in cakes or on wholemeal bread. If you have difficulty finding dried figs, try your local health food shop.

900 g (2 lb) rhubarb
225 g (8 oz) dried figs
rind and juice of one orange and one lemon
1.35 kg (3 lb) sugar

Top and tail the rhubarb and cut it into 12.5-cm (1-in) pieces. Cut up the dried figs into very small pieces. Put the figs in a deep pan with the rhubarb and the grated rind and juice of the orange and lemon. Add the sugar, stir to mix, then leave overnight.

Next day, heat slowly until sugar is dissolved, then boil rapidly until setting point is reached. Allow to cool in the pan for about 20 minutes before putting into clean, warmed jars so that the fruit is distributed evenly throughout. Cover with waxed paper immediately and allow the jam to become really cold before you seal it.

Seville Marmalade

Seville oranges are available during January and February. Their tart flavour makes them ideal for a tangy marmalade.

900 g (2 lb) Seville oranges
2 lemons
4 litres (7 pints) water
1 rounded tablespoon black treacle
2¾ kg (6 lb) sugar

Scrub the fruit well and scald by dropping it into boiling water. Peel and cut up coarsely. Remove the pith from the rinds and put the pith to one side. Cut the rinds into shreds. Put the fruit in a pan with all the pith and pips and half the water. Bring to a boil and simmer gently for about 1½ hours. In a separate pan, put the rind and remaining water. Simmer gently for about 2 hours.

Strain or sieve the fruit and mix with the liquid containing the peel. Stir well to mix and boil off any excess water at this stage, or the marmalade will not set. Add the treacle and sugar. Heat gently until the sugar has dissolved, then boil rapidly until setting point is reached.

Leave to stand for 20 minutes so the peel is evenly distributed, then pour the marmalade into warmed jars. Cover immediately with a waxed disc and seal when cold.

Tomato and Apple Chutney

Give this chutney a peppy taste by adding chilli powder and ginger. Tone it down and use less chilli powder if you prefer your chutney mild.

450 g (1 lb) ripe red tomatoes
450 g (1 lb) cooking apples
225 g ($\frac{1}{2}$ lb) onions
100 g ($\frac{1}{4}$ lb) sultanas
225 g ($\frac{1}{2}$ lb) sugar
1 teaspoon chilli powder
2 good-sized pieces root ginger tied in muslin
salt and pepper
250 ml ($\frac{1}{2}$ pint) vinegar

Skin the tomatoes by dipping them in boiling water for a minute or two. The skins will then peel off quite easily. Peel, core and slice the cooking apples. Chop the onions finely.

Into a large pan (use a preserving pan if you have one) put all the ingredients. Simmer until all the ingredients are blended together and there is no surplus liquid. Remove ginger. Pour at once into hot jars. Seal when cold.

Mixed Mushroom Chutney

1 medium-sized onion
1 medium-sized red pepper
450 g (1 lb) cooking apples
450 g (1 lb) mushrooms
225 g (8 oz) red tomatoes
50 g (2 oz) root ginger
225 g (8 oz) raisins
500 ml (1 pint) vinegar
450 g (1 lb) soft brown sugar

Chop the onion. De-seed the pepper and chop finely. Put both into a pan with 250 ml ($\frac{1}{2}$ pint) water. Simmer to soften. Peel, core and chop the apples. Wash and coarsely chop the mushrooms. Skin the tomatoes by dipping them in boiling water, then cut them up small. Add the apples, mushrooms and tomatoes to the pan and continue cooking. Grate the root ginger and add that. Cook until mixture is 'pulpy'. Add raisins, vinegar and sugar. Stir to mix, then simmer until all the liquid is absorbed—about an hour—stirring from time to time to prevent the mixture sticking.

Pour into hot jars and seal at once.

Rhubarb Chutney

I find the ginger tastes more when not tied in muslin. Leave it loose and fish it out before bottling if you want a stronger flavour.

450 g (1 lb) rhubarb
2 medium-sized onions
225 g (8 oz) soft brown sugar
2 teaspoons curry powder
50 g (2 oz) sultanas
1 teaspoon salt
1 teaspoon pepper
25 g (1 oz) root ginger
250 ml ($\frac{1}{2}$ pint) malt vinegar

Top and tail the rhubarb and cut it into 2.5-cm (1-in) pieces. Chop the onions finely. Put all the ingredients in a thick-based pan (tie the ginger in muslin if you wish). Cook slowly while the onion and rhubarb soften, then boil rapidly until the mixture thickens and any surplus liquid has evaporated. Remove root ginger.

Pour into warmed jars and cover with a waxed disc. Seal when cold. Metal covers must be out of contact with the vinegar, so protect them with wax.

Apple Chutney

A bland chutney which goes well with Cheddar cheese and is ideal for a Ploughman's Lunch.

450 g (1 lb) onions
1.8 kg (4 lb) prepared apples (peeled, cored and chopped)
1 level teaspoon salt
25 g (1 oz) root ginger
2 teaspoons mixed pickling spices
500 ml (1 pint) vinegar
675 g (1$\frac{1}{2}$ lb) sugar
50 g (2 oz) currants

Chop the onions finely and place them in a large heavy pan. Add 250 ml ($\frac{1}{2}$ pint) water. Simmer gently for about 20 minutes. Add the chopped apples, salt with ginger and pickling spices wrapped in muslin. If necessary, add some of the vinegar to prevent apple sticking. Simmer gently until fruit is very soft. Add the sugar, remaining vinegar and currants, then simmer until fruit and vinegar are well blended—about 20 minutes.

Pour into warmed jars and cover with waxed paper. Seal when cold.

Pickled Walnuts

These aren't very cheap to make unless you are lucky enough to know of a tree from which to pick the nuts. However, even if you have to buy the green walnuts at the greengrocer's it's really great fun to try and not at all difficult.

450 g (1 lb) green walnuts
approx 350 g (12 oz) salt
500 ml (1 pint) malt vinegar
25 g (1 oz) pickling spices
2 or 3 pieces root ginger

You must have young green walnuts, picked during June for preference. Wash them and prick all over with a carpet needle or some similar sharp instrument. This is so you can pierce right through the shell and kernel. Dissolve half the salt in 1 litre (2 pints) water and put the walnuts in. Put a weighted plate on top of the water so that the nuts don't float on top.

After five days drain, cover with the rest of the salt dissolved in 1 litre (2 pints) fresh water and leave again for a week. Drain and set the nuts on a baking tray on a sunny window ledge to dry in the sun. They will turn black during this time. Turn them over occasionally so that they colour evenly. Avoid contact with the skin as the juice is by no means easy to remove.

When dry and black pack them in jars. Boil the vinegar with the spices and ginger for ten minutes and allow to cool. Strain the vinegar into the jars and cover the walnuts. Cover and leave for 2–3 months to mature before using.

Pickled Mushrooms

Make the most of mushrooms when they're cheap (often after a weekend), by buying in bulk to make pickles and chutneys.

500 ml (1 pint) vinegar
1 teaspoon mixed pickling spices
450 g (1 lb) mushrooms
salt

Boil the vinegar with the spices, then leave to cool.

152

Pick small mushrooms if you can, or failing that, cut the larger ones in half or quarters. Wash mushrooms and put them in layers in a preserving pan, salting well between each layer. Leave in a warm place for several hours. Stir from time to time.

When the liquor has emerged from the mushrooms, put them into clean jars with a little of the liquor and pour over the spiced vinegar. Cover, seal and leave to mature for about two weeks before use.

Apple Rosemary Jelly

This only makes a small amount of jelly, but double or treble the quantities as you wish. It is excellent with cold lamb or veal.

750 g (1½ lb) cooking apples
250 ml (½ pint) water
1 tablespoon rosemary leaves
2 tablespoons cider vinegar
granulated sugar
few drops green food colouring
sprig of rosemary for decoration

Slice the apples and remove any bad pieces. Put them in a saucepan with the water, rosemary leaves and cider vinegar. Cook slowly until the apples are completely soft. In the meantime scald a jelly bag or some kind of muslin. Pour the pulp into the bag and suspend it over another container. I usually suspend the jelly bag over a bucket (which has been well scalded) by tying the bag firmly to a long-handled wooden spoon placed across the top. Cover and allow to drip overnight. Don't squeeze the pulp or you will end up with a cloudy jelly.

Next day measure the juice in a measuring jug and add 225 g (8 oz) sugar to every 250 ml (½ pint) of juice. Pour sugar and juice into a saucepan with a few drops of green food colouring. Heat gently at first to dissolve the sugar, then boil rapidly until setting point is reached.

If you have a sugar thermometer it's easy, because you boil to 104°C (220°F). Otherwise boil for about ten minutes then test by removing a teaspoon of the jelly and putting it on a cold saucer. If it is ready it will set quickly and wrinkle on the surface if pushed with the finger.

Pour into a hot jar, curl a sprig of rosemary on top. Cover with waxed paper, allow to cool, then cover in the usual way.

Crab Apple Jelly

This is superb with lamb or hare, and you can use it for sponge cakes too, so it really is a versatile preserve.

2 kg (4½ lb) crab apples
1½ litres (2¼ pints) water
sugar

Wash the crab apples and remove any bruised or blemished parts. Put them into a large pan with the water and bring to the boil. Simmer until the apples are very soft.

Strain through a jelly bag suspended over a bucket or similar container that has been scalded with boiling water, and allow the juice to drip through overnight. Don't be tempted to squeeze the pulp or the jelly will be cloudy.

Measure the juice and to every 500 ml (1 pint) add 450 g (1 lb) sugar. Dissolve the sugar in the juice, then boil rapidly until setting point is reached, removing any scum during the boiling. Test jelly, and if ready pour into clean dry jars, cool and seal.

Index